SPIRITUAL POWER

SPIRITUAL POWER
Being and Becoming

Volume 1

Gian Kumar

HAY HOUSE INDIA

New Delhi • London • Sydney
Carlsbad, California • New York City

Hay House Publishers (India) Pvt. Ltd.
Muskaan Complex, Plot No.3, B-2 Vasant Kunj, New Delhi-110 070, India
Hay House Inc., PO Box 5100, Carlsbad, CA 92018-5100, USA
Hay House UK, Ltd., The Sixth Floor, Watson House, 54 Baker Street, W1U 7BU, UK
Hay House Australia Pty Ltd., 18/36 Ralph St., Alexandria NSW 2015, Australia

Email: contact@hayhouse.co.in
www.hayhouse.co.in

Copyright © 2023 Gian Kumar

The views and opinions expressed in this book are the author's own and the facts are as reported by him. They have been verified to the extent possible, and the publishers are not in any way liable for the same.

All rights reserved. No part of this publication may be reproduced, by any mechanical, photographic, or electronic process, or in the form of a phonographic recording, nor may it be stored in a retrieval system, transmitted, or otherwise be copied for public or private use – other than for 'fair use' as brief quotations embodied in articles and reviews – without prior written permission of the publisher.

The author of this book does not dispense medical advice or prescribe the use of any technique as a form of treatment for physical, emotional, or medical problems without the advice of a physician, either directly or indirectly. The intent of the author is only to offer information of a general nature to help you in your quest for emotional and spiritual well-being. In the event you use any of the information in this book for yourself – which is your constitutional right – the author and the publisher assume no responsibility for your actions.

ISBN 978-93-86832-17-7
ISBN 978-93-86832-18-4 (e-book)

To
All Spiritual Beings

Contents

Preface 9

Chapter 1	A Balance in Life	17
Chapter 2	Body, Mind and Spirit	26
Chapter 3	The Power of the Mind	38
Chapter 4	How We See Ourselves	46
Chapter 5	The Purpose of Life	51
Chapter 6	Seeking Enlightenment	60
Chapter 7	Three Techniques of Meditation	68
Chapter 8	The Need for a Guru	75
Chapter 9	What Is Reality?	86
Chapter 10	Enjoying Life: Slow and Steady	92
Chapter 11	Spiritual but Not Religious	101
Chapter 12	The Power of Language	108
Chapter 13	The Pursuit of Silence	114
Chapter 14	The Mind and Its Awareness	122

Chapter 15	Are We Intellectuals?	130
Chapter 16	The Flow of Life	136
Chapter 17	The Flow of Energy	142
Chapter 18	Here and Now	153
Chapter 19	Life … a Paradox	161
Chapter 20	The Power of the Spirit	169
Chapter 21	What Is the Soul: 1?	179
Chapter 22	What Is the Soul? 2	189
Chapter 23	Awakening of the Soul – Kundalini	198
Chapter 24	Personal Power	207
Chapter 25	Life … What a Delusion!	217
Chapter 26	The Meaning of Life and Death	227
Chapter 27	In Search of Ourselves	236
Chapter 28	The Concept of Completeness	247
Chapter 29	Awareness Is Everything	258
Chapter 30	The Importance of Self-Realization	272

Author's Note	285
Acknowledgements	286

Preface

The state of our becoming is far more important than the state of our being.

— Gian Kumar

For me, it is in the space within my inner self where I find solace. It has taken me the better part of the last decade to realize that whatever I am searching for is right here. My intense research into the subject of spirituality, over the years, took me through innumerable books, lectures, videos, discourses and gurus, until finally, the truth dawned on me. My search was over. Why do we need to seek the light of enlightenment *outside* of ourselves? All the while it is shining bright within. This book gives insights on how we can spiritually empower ourselves to discover this hidden illumination.

Life is but a dream; we all want something out of everything. On the one hand, our mind is designed for developing the ego, yearns for material acquisitions and is obsessed with attachments; it clings to the body mesmerized by thoughts of 'me, mine and myself'. On the other hand, we claim to be honest, religious, kind-hearted, generous and what not. In this realm of hypocrisy, there is a constant war of conflicting emotions that we wage against ourselves. Soon, the mind gets conditioned to child-like beliefs; creating a fear within us that God will punish us, if we do this or that.

The irony is we remain confused in spite of attaining so much knowledge through various sources. We have created Gods – some divine beings above ourselves: is this out of fear, insecurity, arrogance, or a sense of superiority that my God is more benevolent than yours? Or is God just in our minds? We all have divinity within; seek and ye shall find (as stated in the Bible).

It seems we just do not know what truth is all about; nor are we true to ourselves. Love and truth are the most carelessly used words and grossly misunderstood by us. We use the word love liberally for all those we are sentimental about. The truth within us has no depth as it keeps changing over time, and also differs in its meaning vis-à-vis every individual. Many of us just don't have the guts to face the real truth and its reality. Such truth hurts our ego and self-esteem to the extent that we are ready to delude and deceive others, and also ourselves, as long as our ego is fed and remains inflated.

***

Now, we come to the crucial question: What is *spiritual power*? In my view, it is that inner awareness and the capability to awaken our mind and to get rid of the ignorant notion that we are solely body and mind, but something more. What exactly is that something more, which makes us who we are? Our consciousness, in order to recognize this truth, has been empowered with *spiritual awareness* to experience and realize the self and its relationship with the universe.

This awareness is empowering because it enables us to know who and what we really are and the purpose of our existence on this earth. The lessons we learn, and our experiences and realizations on this spiritual journey, empower us with that added energy to pursue the goal of fulfilment in life where there is a balance with regard to the material and the spiritual.

Spiritual awareness can lead us to that completeness in life, which we all yearn for. Spiritual empowerment provides us that access to a journey within ourselves in search for the ultimate reality and its truth. However, the most crucial factor on this aspect of awareness is that it empowers us to become aware of our own thoughts, feelings and actions. We keep analysing and judging others, not giving any consideration to the inner functioning of our mind.

***

How *real* is reality? Do we see it as it is, or as we perceive it? Our minds, cluttered as they are, create their own realities; our past experiences influence these realities to a large extent. Only the true nature of reality cannot be distorted. It exists as it is, whether our sensory organs agree or not. So the ultimate reality of life is to be one with the universe, overcoming all our differences. This is the aim of spirituality, going beyond the mind–body connection into a spiritual realm, where all that exists is only one and not two.

***

Both science and religion have not been able to fathom the basis of our consciousness or the need for the 'soul'. As a result, due to the religions we follow, our minds are conditioned by a variety of beliefs, dogmas and superstitions. And with science constantly moving its goal posts, doubting and challenging everything, there is no finality to our reality.

Though it may sound odd, science and spirituality are compatible; in recent times even die-hard scientists have accepted this as the gospel truth. For instance, Carl Sagan (1934–1996)* once said: 'The notion that science and spirituality are somehow mutually exclusive does a disservice to both.'

***

This book marks a progressive series from my three previous books,** clarifying the subject of spiritualism in its true actuality, without blending into any religion whatsoever. I am not pointing to anything new or to something beyond our capability. In our journey from the self to the Self, we should question every belief that our mind commands, before finalizing the best route, commencing from materialism and moving towards spiritualism.

***

My books neither offer preaching, mantras or enlightenment nor are they based upon any archaic or dogmatic doctrines or precepts. For that, we have enough orthodox preachers and so-called 'gurus' regurgitating every day, what has been narrated for centuries, in different versions. In my opinion, spirituality simply revolves around one word: 'Oneness'. How complex have

---

*An American astronomer, cosmologist, astrophysicist, astrobiologist, author and science communicator.
**1. *Know Thyself*, Leadstart Publishing, Mumbai, 2015. 2. *Think from the Heart and Love from the Mind*, Leadstart Publishing, Mumbai, 2015. 3. *The Ultimate Reality*, Leadstart Publishing, Mumbai, 2015.

we have made, both in worldly and spiritual existence, this one simple word!

***

The reason for writing this book is also to reveal the hollowness with which our conditioned mind is influenced by the factors carefully inscribed into various chapters. I have written on diverse topics that are related to our daily existence. In each chapter, I have delved deep into the topic, which may seem complex at times, but is essential for us to know and understand. I am sure if we are in tune with the subject, we will appreciate and gain something from its content.

My books are meant for serious spiritual seekers who wish to balance their life, the material with the spiritual, considering them as one whole and not separate. You need not read this book in a sequential order, as each chapter is based on a different topic. But when you read, you may have to go through each chapter more than once, in order to pause and contemplate on the intensity behind each written thought. Many readers may stop to ponder over the contents, in order to reflect on what they have read. Please do so; the process shall provide stimulus to awaken you from the slumber induced by the rituals of conditioned thinking.

***

The spirit of what I wish to convey is beyond words and, in the inner dimensions, beyond thoughts. The words here are only meant to point towards the direction that each one of us has to follow, one day or the other. If these words are in coherence with your inner self, please allow my books to do their work, which is to steer you away from blind beliefs and conditioned thinking, transforming your inner self and transcending the consciousness with awareness. Today, this is no longer a luxury, but a necessity.

Please keep on questioning every thought that comes to your mind, asking if that is really true or not; your mind will refuse to give you a straight answer. The mind is too clever and smart. It will never reveal the truth through words or thoughts, interpreting the same with varying changes, which are emotionally or psychologically influenced only in self-interest. The truth, in fact, can be experienced and realized, *only* by your own self.

***

In this volume, I have attempted to answer many queries, which may trouble the mind during the course of a lifetime by sharing my thoughts with you the readers. You may not concur with each and every one of my answers; but if I have set you thinking on the spiritual path, then that would serve my purpose of writing the book.

***

I would like to point out that repetitions, in the spiritual context, are unavoidable since the concepts are infinite while the words to describe them remain pitifully finite. In my books, I have constantly used concepts and words such as absolute, oneness, energy, self and so on. Besides, intellectually, I have kept in mind the reader's need to understand and absorb the subject, step by step. Hence, the repetition of core ideas at each juncture helps the message to be distilled and internalized, instead of remaining partially understood.

It does not necessarily follow that the reader should agree with everything written. When the mind becomes impatient or restless, signalling it has understood, the reader should move on. The subjects/chapters often revolve around words such as 'awareness' or 'oneness', which stand like the basic scale a classical raga is based on. Thereupon, myriad variations and nuances are played out, to attempt to convey the numerous extensions possible within the same theme.

The serious seeker of spirituality returns by compulsion, to read again and again and hear those notes as a recurring melody, until the theme becomes clear. Like chanting a mantra, he* then gains the proper perspective to practise what he has read.

— Gian Kumar

---

*In this book, there is no gender bias intended; the 'he' could well be a 'she'.

Chapter 1

A Balance in Life

Life is like riding a bicycle. To keep your balance, you must keep moving.
— Albert Einstein*

If people were asked the question as to what is most important to them in life, very few would give the answer as balance. Most of us either underestimate the significant role of balance in our lives or we are not aware of its contribution. The young normally take this phenomenon lightly; the middle-aged take it for granted; and the elderly have to face the brunt with regard to those factors or aspects, which they had earlier ignored or neglected.

***

Our whole universe can survive, sustain itself and remain stabilized only if everything is *balanced*. Equilibrium may be difficult to support for long but it is that upright balance and stability, which are essential. Life too is but

---

*Albert Einstein (14 March 1879 to 18 April 1955) was a German-born theoretical physicist. His theory of relativity and his influence on the philosophy of science made him pre-eminent all over the world. He bagged the 1921 Nobel Prize for physics.

a balance of factors as diverse as discipline, rhythm, control, elegance and harmony – existentially and experientially.

We need not run after balance; we just need to be aware and conscious. The moment we start to think how to balance ourselves in life, the rest will follow. There is no extra effort to be made; all that is required is to allocate our potentialities and self-manage in accordance with our priorities. The art of life is to experientially balance our mind, body and spirit in the right manner. The process starts when our thoughts inwardly create a strong relationship with our own mind and body.

***

Thinking refers to the motion of the psychic energy within the mind. The problem we face is that the mind, when it goes into motion, can think only in terms of duality: relating with opposites. The mind separates the oneness of this energy into its extremes. It refuses to stay in the centre, for it is easy for the mind to shift from one position to another, say, from happiness to sadness, but difficult to remain calm and tranquil. In the centre, where there is balance, there too we have movement, but it is by accepting both the opposites with equal grace.

As just stated, life is a balance between the internal and the external, the material and the spiritual, where it constantly expands and evolves but never concludes. When life concludes, beliefs become rigid. The mind habitually ends up choosing in self-interest after tilting from one side to another. However, the energy of life constantly remains in the centre: both God and the devil, positive and negative, are just two sides of the same coin. Without the former, the latter wouldn't exist. All that exists is only one and not two; it is the mind, which separates the same into a duality in order to choose, analyse, discern and utilize for its own needs.

We should never cling to any one duality because nothing is permanent. What is good to us may not be to another. Both happiness and sadness are inherent and intrinsic to each other as one. Take the case of a tightrope walker. He balances the ends of a pole to remain poised in spite of the restriction in the area of movement. If he leans a little more towards one side, he will need to correct that by bending to the other side. One has to adjust both ends with the help of a pole, converging the weight of the mass to be centred on that rope. This is a perfect example of how to centralize and balance our polarities.

We need to be alert, aware and poised throughout our life, for nothing is simple and easy. We just cannot avoid and ignore one aspect of existence over another. Just because we choose, say, one friend over someone else, this does not give us the right to ignore the other; we need to be fair to all. The balance can be towards any particular centre, which is not a point or a fixed position. The action is more of balancing, say, in the middle of any two polarities, as close to each other as possible. For instance, both good and bad are inseparable: what is profitable for us may not be for another person. We need to accept both views and balance the two, bringing about harmony for all.

Moreover, staying in the middle for long is also difficult. We have to make a constant effort; we keep tilting under emotions, desires and attachments from one side to another. We should try to be like a tightrope walker: regain and retain our balance and remain poised. The centre is alive and dynamic; we need to be steady and experience that again and again. It is vibrant and lively in whatever situation we may find ourselves; both ends require their respective attention with awareness and with equanimity and grace.

***

Life gives us both happiness and sadness; we have to accept both with respect and grace, experiencing and realizing both with awareness. If one is present, the other is not too far; the effort should be to remain in the middle and become receptive to both. This art of balancing between any two polarities is the secret of life. The mind should be alert and focused; whichever way circumstances may take us, we should be energetic and alive.

***

We should not allow the mind to make us regret this event or that, either concerning the past or dreaming about the future. When every moment of life is continuously changing, how can we remain stationary? Equilibrium can be attained only briefly; it is balance, which keeps rotating around the centre point, like a spinning top.

A wise person will experience both joy and sorrow with awareness and know his limitations vis-à-vis balance. All dualities exist within the same field of any force in any source of energy. For example, the force of electricity remains constant, but separating the field into positive and negative activates it. The field of energy dances in duality: in the absence of light there is darkness, even though the force of energy is singular and constant. However, its field requires changes in polarity to create motion and to move away from its fixed state of equilibrium, creating a ground for the spirit or energy to play.

The job of a human mind is to separate the force of aware energy in order to become conscious, choose from different options and ensure self-preservation. We should always remember that the prime aspect, which separates us (human beings and animals) from all other objects of matter, is that we are conscious of what we do and the rest are not.

***

When one end of duality is given more importance due to self-interest, it creates a disturbance in the overall equilibrium of that oneness of energy. Since both combine to form one, it is our inner state of awareness, which counters this imbalance, guiding us towards the art of balancing. This separation of energy is required for us to experience both staying awake and sleeping. We have to experience both; the problem arises when we start clinging to one, forgetting the other.

When this happens, life becomes chaotic and disturbed; opposites are required to understand, experience and realize what balancing for regaining that oneness is all about. This happens to be the basic purpose of life. The aware energy within our mind keeps flowing from one duality to another; it is the degree of individual balancing, which determines the quality and state of our life. The rational needs to be balanced with the irrational; only then can we find some concrete answers. The other part must not be ignored.

In the same manner, science needs to be balanced with spirituality, with the outer experiencing the inner. Science relies on the objectivity of physical existence; spirituality enters the subject of life. The outer perception requires balancing with that inner awareness, which is purely the nature of reality in the presence of that moment. It is from one that we understand the other. For instance, we may enjoy perfect health and have all the wealth, besides family and friends in our material existence, but if we ignore the inner spirit, that subject within, there will always be something amiss and we will remain imbalanced. What is inside is nothing but a continuum with the outside.

***

The art of balancing physically, mentally, emotionally, financially, socially and spiritually in terms of our existence as a whole may sound easy. Internal balancing requires constant rhythm in dynamism with vibrant energy. When we practise the art of balancing, it increases the presence of our mind, from one moment to the next in all our actions. It requires consistent awareness in a state of alert watchfulness, where we may need to alter and re-alter ourselves according to any situation, constantly changing while experiencing life with every passing minute.

***

The whole secret lies in gaining awareness of why, what and how the presence of our being reflects the human embodiment. Yoga, meditation with mindfulness and controlled breathing are some of the techniques useful in the art of balancing the body, the mind and the spirit. They direct us towards totality in fulfilment, completeness and well-being in our life.

When it comes to our body, physiological balance is possible only with help of the psychological element and the same, in turn, is balanced by the spiritual. The causes of most diseases are largely attributed to imbalances in the interactions between multiple energy systems of the body. These imbalances create leakages, causing depletion in our overall movement of energy. Our body responds to the way we think, feel and act. If the mind is agitated or excited, our body will react to that emotional disturbance, say, through erratic blood pressure or improper digestion.

Again, dealing with stress, anxiety or depression for maintaining our physical and mental health requires proper balancing. Not only that, today science is telling us we need to have a balance also with the human microbiota, those trillions of microscopic creatures surrounding our eyes, ears, guts and so on. We are, in fact, ecosystems living in balance with a whole community of microbes that surround us. They play a role not only in optimizing our health but also in influencing our behaviour and personality.

Instead of emotionally reacting, if correct thoughts are rationally supported with the right action, we are considered to be in psychological balance. Again, on this tightrope, we have a crossover between the mental, the spiritual (plus the emotional*), which requires further balancing. Creating this balance spiritually, and acquiring that power, is what this book is all about. We need to exercise the right balance between the two to remain in peace with joy, which is that answer to life. We also need to have control over our mind and body not by renouncing, but also not tilting towards any particular direction weighed down by desire, emotions or circumstances.

***

Spirituality connects us to the source of everything. It relates to consciousness, mindfulness and oneness. A human being outwardly may be defined by his deeds, but

---

*The emotional aspect is an unconscious movement of thought driven purely for interacting in self-interest, whereas awareness is that pristine energy, which awakens the mind consciously to know the actual nature of reality.

it is his experiential self that defines the completeness in totality. Behind his experiences are those subtle thoughts that lead him to a greater reality. It is this understanding in awareness that takes him towards the balance of all three factors in consonance with the outside world.

***

Life is but an experience of dualities in physicality, balancing the ego self with the witnessing self. If we wish for completeness, fulfilment and well-being, we need to go deep within ourselves to achieve the balance between the personal and the impersonal consciousness: between the ego and the divine. Such a 'journey' shall provide us with correct thoughts, actions, experiences and their realization, not only for ourselves but also for the world around us.

***

The significance of spiritual power supersedes the length of this chapter. However, if we consider all the above factors in totality, only then will we be able to comprehend the depth of experiencing and realizing the processes engendered by spirituality. We may not have control over circumstances, since we are dependent upon external factors. However, we definitely have the power to exercise the self in the manner that we choose. This inner self is referred to as the spirit, consciousness or soul, which has been defined and explained in the minutest detail in order to empower us on a safe journey in this chaotic world.

***

You the reader will not be able to capture the essence of this book merely by casual reading. This book is more of a study; you may begin from any chapter, but certain sections will require more than one read. You also need to read slowly and carefully, because the basic understanding of any insightful knowledge is not because it is simply been put forth, but it requires to be effectively hammered into our wavering mind filled with blind beliefs.

Chapter 2

BODY, MIND AND SPIRIT

Health is a state of complete harmony of the body, mind and spirit. When one is free from physical disabilities and mental distractions, the gates of the soul open.

— B. K. S. Iyengar[*]

What exactly do we mean by the oft-used phrase: body, mind and spirit or mind, body and spirit? From psychology to religion to spirituality, we carelessly use these words in a light manner, without bothering to know in depth their meaning and as to why these three components are used as one in totality. Here, I present a deeper understanding of these entities so that we may awaken to know, understand and experience all three in a composite manner for the benefit of our total well-being.

The trio of body, mind and spirit indicates that our energy system can be ascribed to three distinct layers, or forms, expanding and evolving in their respective attributes, but, by itself, remaining as one in totality.

---

[*]B. K. S. Iyengar (14 December 1918 to 20 August 2014) was considered one of the foremost yoga teachers in the world. He has written many books on yoga practice and philosophy.

Let us start with the body and probe deeper into the currents of how these three different forms of energies communicate in the physical, mental and spiritual spheres.

The reason to understand the oneness of the three components arises because there are some who limit themselves only to bodily pleasures. There are also many, who unconsciously remain trapped in their ego, living mostly for mental appeasement. It is only when our energy currents are disturbed, leaking or diminishing, we find something amiss and wake up and inquire as to how do we rectify the faults?

***

In simple terms, the mind influences the body and the spirit the mind. A proper balancing is imperative, otherwise the stress and uncertainty of life today would throw us into an abyss. We go on sinking, inviting ailments and diseases out of fear to anxiety to depression. If we wish to maintain harmony and health, a series of methods relating to all three entities in proper coordination should be taken into account. We are required to follow them diligently, so that modern-day stresses that affect the mind do not disturb the communication of the three components with each other. A combination of a sound body, a rational mind and a compassionate soul is what we require.

The body on its own possesses an amazingly strong defence mechanism to look after itself, so long as the mind does not interfere and distract it from its rhythm of functioning. The body has its own biological intelligence to counter any attacks, either from the environment or elsewhere (say, physical abuse). Without asking the mind, it automatically carries on its repair job, provided the mind is asleep or tranquil. The problem arises when the mind keeps on demanding more and more out of life, resulting in emotions such as anger, agitation, greed, envy, jealousy, contempt and hatred leading to anxiety, fear, depression and suffering. All these outbursts have a direct impact on the body simply because of the body and mind being connected to each other as one.

Therefore, during childhood, when the mind is less assertive, the body looks after itself without requiring much help either from the mind or the spirit. However, during adulthood, the psychological intelligence of the brain increases and the mind takes over to rule in the manner that it thinks fit. The ego reigns supreme, creating constant chaos within the mind. The psychic intelligence becomes reckless with no one to control it. There is no captain to navigate the ship of the body and the mind, since most of us are incapable of handling our ego. The stress that follows slows down our energy transmissions making the system sluggish, causing irreparable damage both to the body as well as to the mind.

This mental agony becomes a regular feature, resulting in insecurity, when we struggle to somehow control our circumstances. Our brooding thoughts continue to focus more on the past and future, hardly able to enjoy the present. We turn restless and irritable. We sometimes become miserable due to anger engendered by a bloated ego; we tend to boast about our glorious past or may begin to desire excessively something or the other in the future. Our psychic intelligence gets impaired and suppresses the biological intelligence from doing its own job with its involuntary motions.

What is the use of this intellectuality if it cannot serve its purpose at the right time and place to show us the proper direction? In fact, basic commonsense should tell us that now the moment has arrived for us to search for that missing third factor, which will control this incessant anxiety and disquiet. We reach that stage when our ego, which was earlier constructive in our ensuring peace and happiness, has gone to our head. In other words, it is now that we require the third ingredient (the spirit) to control the ego and keep it under check.

Unfortunately, at this stage, most of us start running helter-skelter seeking external assistance from others' experiences. However, there are a few of us who proactively take charge of this shaky situation and transform ourselves. The third entity emerges; the spiritual quotient lying dormant within awakens and connects our body and mind with that ultimate ingredient, balancing all three in one composite unit. It is to attain this spiritual empowerment that we now embark on a thorough study, going through innumerable pages and referring to numerous other sources to understand the meaning of life.

***

The spirit silently witnesses all that the body and mind go through unless it is awakened to govern and regulate the manner in which it wishes the mind to perform. During the initial witnessing stage, the spirit softly whispers and guides, whenever our mind crosses any limit, warning us of its outcome. It keeps itself dormant until the moment we become aware and open our eyes to look inwards rather than outwards. What we seek lies within; all we require is that spiritual awakening to arouse our inner self, the real us and not the mind, to experience the divinity of what we are.

The mind awakens by getting rid of this ignorance that we are not body and mind, which we thought ourselves to be. There exists a serene absolute intelligence, referred to as the spirit, lying dormant within our mind, witnessing all that is happening. The presence of that spirit enables us to observe, read, check, navigate and control our own mind.

What we really need to know at this point is how to become aware of our own inner thoughts. It becomes irrefutable that we are not the mind but the controller and navigator of the same. It is the spirit, which goes through subjective experiences, that makes the mind experience its objectivity. This aspect is beyond science, because like the mind, scientific experiences are based upon what it can observe and infer physically and objectively. The subject of life hence remains within the sphere of spirituality to experience and realize what divine consciousness is all about.

***

The fundamental difference, which sets us apart from all other objects, is that we as humans are conscious of all that we think about, indulge in and experience, whereas others are not. These conscious experiences from the memory gradually accumulate to form our unique self-consciousness. This phenomenon is superior to anything that we know and is also everything to us. Without this self-consciousness, we will not be in any way different from any other object existing in this world. It is primarily for this reason it is pertinent for us to know the subject of life in order to learn, understand, experience and realize who, what and how we are.

The understanding of this concept initiates a new aura of intelligence. If properly understood and experienced, it can connect all the three forms of energies in body, mind and spirit together as one. It can give us the personal power to know that health (of the body), wealth (from the mind) and wisdom (spiritual realization) are equally essential to life in their sequential order.

***

All three, body, mind and spirit, are interconnected and a balance among these three can provide that solace and tranquillity, which we seek in life. Research, time and again, has shown how our physiological, psychological and spiritual health has a direct link to our overall well-being. None of them can be sustained without the other, as they all constitute the same unitary indivisible energy, contributing different attributes.

We may have all the wealth and spiritual wisdom in the world, but if our body is not in tune with the mind or if it is not looked after properly, life is not worth its physical existence. The spirit being the core energy of our inner self and the mind subtle energy, both reside in the gross mass that is the body. Meaning, the real us, if awakened can do wonders with a healthy body, an alert mind and the right spiritual attitude. It is only the human mind, which has the ability to awaken that divine spirit, embodied within, by becoming aware of its own degree of awareness.

***

The East, from prehistoric times, has been advocating the same unison, defining in one word all three: yoga. Furthermore, with the rapid advancement in scientific studies, the linkage among body, mind and spirit has become stronger. Science itself advocates self-healing as a valid tool. Our lifestyle patterns – during sleep, handling stress, dieting, exercise, proper breathing, taking health supplements, meditation and yoga – all have an impact on our inner world of thoughts, emotions, desires and choices. Today, science for the outer world and spirituality for the inner one are coming closer to each other for the betterment of humanity.

***

The spirit, with proper insight, perceives and reflects the outer world, navigates the mind to bring out the difference between the truth and falsehood. It does not give any justifications or judgements from an egoist mind. However, the mind still remains the ultimate medium, the instrument through which it is eventually made possible to stabilize all three and combine them into one. The mind is also designed to separate its energy into relativity in dichotomies, because the material energy of desire activates the experiencing self of the mind. This desire makes the mind relate one dual form to another in order to choose via intellect; reasoning in self-interest on what it should indulge in and experience. The realization of this enters the memory bank and becomes a crucial part of our 'remembering' self. It is through this remembrance that we remain conscious to know who, what and how we are to interact in the spheres of both the material and the spiritual.

The mind plays its role making us aware: at one end, the ego functioning in duality and, at the other, the witnessing self, directing us on how to counter any negative effects. All this can have a substantial effect only if we are true to our own selves. We will need to answer truthfully spiritual questions like: Is the ego still persisting in false self-identification or are we sublime with that oneness all around?

***

Spirituality has three different connotations. The first is towards religion and the second when going off at a tangent towards God realization, past life transgression, afterlife and the eternity of consciousness. The third is more towards logic, rationality and its experiential analysis. It involves the universality of that one and only ingredient, the spirit, which prevails over and pervades all that exists in this universe. We only live once; so we should make the most of our life. We come from nothing – from the dark energy of the universe – and go back into nothing. All that we leave behind are memories to remember us by. (This concept shall be discussed in greater detail in one of my forthcoming books.)

***

The confusion or conflict arises when a spiritual seeker is not clear in what manner he wishes his spiritual self to evolve: religious through God realization or in forming his devotional individuality for eternity.

The words spirit and spirituality are so liberally used today that all of us simply seem to know how spiritual we are. Intellectually, we may be certain of what we know; however, experientially we reveal our ignorance. First, we must observe and know our own selves and only then, with awareness of every moment, experience and realize whether we are spiritual or not.

In many cases, we will be surprised to know that even spiritual artistes try to market their persona to prove to others their spiritual acumen. Because of this false mask covering the spirit, we find hypocrisy all around. Spirituality is a pure internal experience wherein we realize our own selves; we can find the spirit in our acts of godliness filled with compassion and love in the divine self for all, as one.

The difficulty arises because spirituality demands living in the non-dual form; the cognitive mind is fundamentally designed for the dual form. Both reside in the brain: the former in the presence of that supreme absolute awareness and the latter in the presence of relating everything in opposites, mainly desiring self-interest for the sake of self-identification, called ego. We have to surrender one to acquire the other. Only the mind can decide as to which path to undertake: the one towards the absolute truth in oneness or the one leading to playing around in duality, telling lies to itself, presuming and claiming to be devoid of ego, which generally is not the case.

It is for this reason that spirituality claims that, in the absolute world, there are no words to explain God, love, reality, truth, now and so on. These are only experiences for the mind to get the taste of the absolute. The practice, experience and realization of spirituality are possible only through silence and not through words. The mind will only come up with numerous concepts, one to be overruled by another. No words spoken or written by anybody can take us to the destination called spirituality; they can, at the most, only point us towards that direction.

***

The mind may analyse everything through scientific knowledge and reasoning, but falters when emotional outbursts interfere. Always remember: the body is existential; the mind is intellectual; and the spirit is experiential. The spirit has to bypass the analytical dual mind and express through the body what it wishes to convey. Therefore, we should never ignore the body in which both the mind and the soul reside. We may not notice it, but the body subtly reveals everything to a keen observer, which we ourselves may not know.

Therefore, we should, besides the mind, listen to, and rely on, the body too. The body has ways and means of communicating on many occasions more than what the analytical mind can through its thinking. The body reaps what the mind and the spirit sow. It can exhibit the flow of the mind and the spirit so exuberantly with grace and love for all to see.

As far as the mind is concerned, we should not only listen to it but also tame it. The mind has two distinct sections: the lower and the upper. The lower section deals with analysing, processing and experiencing thoughts. This is done by choosing, reasoning, discerning and indulging. Gradually, within this memory section, the storehouse of our experiences, the upper part develops. We become the ones who remember, forming our consciousness and, with the aid of the witnessing mind, we perceive the inner self. The body and the mind in due course of time disintegrate, but due to the presence of the absolute witnessing self – that remembering self – the inner spirit rises. We mature, leaving behind our individuality as a legacy, when we are no longer there.

This individual spirit is that presence of our being that forms our individuality, summing up 'who' we are. The self-consciousness forms the content of our remembering mind as to 'what' we are. The body in which both reside reveals 'how' we are. This spirit internally perceives what goes around within, directing, guiding and controlling the mind. The lower mind, through its sensory organs, perceives externally the material world and forms our personality. The higher mind, through inner perception, becomes responsible for developing our individuality through our consciousness.

The lower mind depends on its intellect, based on past knowledge, and acts mainly in self-interest. The higher mind is related to the awareness of both the inner and the outer and spontaneously functions with intuitiveness. The lower mind gives rise to false, illusory sensations of supremacy leading towards ego, which makes us feel separate and distant from others. It is purely guided by desires for personal satisfaction creating a false self, eventually dragging us into the web of fear, anxiety and suffering.

At this point, spiritual awareness intervenes and informs us that we are more than our physical identities of gender, race, profession, religion and nationality. It is at this stage of life we connect our body and mind to the spirit by moving towards that inner power and attaining experiential knowledge of how to remain stable with truth, love and positivity.

This spiritual strength can gather speed only if and when we come to know with conviction that we are more than just the body and the cognitive mind. We are that presence of our awareness, which oversees everything. First we need to see by observing, to believe with conviction and, after that, 'be with it' experientially. This procedure shall prove to our body and mind that peace and joy can be realized in the presence of that spirit, which flows in continuum within all that exists, as one and not two.

***

For connecting the spirit to our body and mind, we need to derive knowledge from the theory of spiritualism, practise those methods provided by spirituality and become spiritual by virtue of our deeds and not words, compassionately in oneness. We will then connect the body, the mind and the spirit not only with the internal self but also with the external spirit in continuum as one.

***

Though the mind is everything for us, it requires proper handling, which can be done only if our spirit awakens to take over our mind. Meaning: when we come to know how to become aware of our own past awareness. The outer perception of existing with duality takes us towards separation from one extreme to the other and negatively towards the totality in general. As a result of these negative vibrations, our thoughts become responsible for the intensifying emotions of fear, anxiety, jealousy and contempt, leaving us perturbed and confused.

Spirituality guides us in many ways through yoga how to counter the negative aspects of the mind. However, the most vital factor is to first recognize and acknowledge the inner truth. The truth of who and what we are, and also, most importantly, admitting to that truth without any justification, when our mind functions in an egoist manner. This becomes possible when, instead of blindly believing and following what we are told, we use our commonsense, think methodically, are rational and do not judge by comparing ourselves to anybody else.

We should proceed in the journey of life by providing the right connectivity of all these three forms of energies to enhance their effectiveness and fulfilment. We should remember that the outer world is nothing but a reflection of our own consciousness, the manner in which we experience and realize life. All we need to do is to bring grace, gratitude and godliness, which will definitely reveal one day whether our body, mind and spirit are in consonance or not.

Chapter 3

THE POWER OF THE MIND

We are not human beings having a spiritual experience. We are spiritual beings having a human experience.
— Pierre Teilhard de Chardin*

The universe is considered to be a sea of aware energy where forces with interchangeable energies vibrate in different frequencies, which, when condensed, exhibit themselves through various forms. Similarly, a human brain is one such source of power. Thoughts too comprise a form of energy, transmitting its vibrating power in different frequencies and directing us towards a chosen outcome. Raw energy is manifested, stored and transmitted by the mind through separate intellectual, emotional, physical and spiritual fields, making us aware and conscious to experience life.

Let us follow the spiritual path, which the mind through its exclusive power undertakes to create as it evolves from its lower to its higher consciousness. The mind separates the field of aware energy into two distinct

---

*Pierre Teilhard de Chardin (1 May 1881 to 10 April 1955) was a French idealist philosopher and priest, besides being a scientist.

entities: material and spiritual. The manner an individual mind utilizes and transforms power from the lower to the higher consciousness determines its level of aliveness and effectiveness.

The material aspect is consciously transmitted by thoughts to the other centres of the mind more in self-interest and for the sake of self-preservation; the thoughts may revolve around desires and attachments. The mind separates the absoluteness of the aware energy into its duality, in order to distinguish one from the other and to choose from opposites what it desires to experience and indulge in. In this way, the mind, while experiencing both ends of duality, develops a form of self-consciousness, which it absorbs through its level of awareness.

The mind, in actuality, is basically a mechanical machine, which requires awareness to kick-start its operations. The presence of this awareness makes the mind conscious, a factor that differs from one individual to another. It is awareness that rules the mind and makes it expand, evolve and transform – within the sphere of its own qualities – in order to form its individuality.

***

The material mind revolves around desires and attachments and the spiritual side goes towards completeness, compassion and connectedness. The material mind has the power to think, whereas the spiritual mind watches and witnesses what the material mind is thinking. The spiritual is the subject of which the material mind becomes as a part of its objective to undertake the journey of life.

***

If there is any power greater than our ego, it is that level of spiritual power, which we often ignore. Humankind has always been fascinated with this spiritual power. I prefer referring to that as *our own personal power*. We normally think that it is our cognitive mind, which is in control of everything, but, in reality it is the level of our innate intelligence, the presence of our being and the quality of awareness, which holds the real power within us. This inner intelligence makes our mind conscious, connecting the primordial awareness to evolve from ego consciousness and move towards the divine. Both the material and the spiritual co-exist, whether they are in accord or not, and are intrinsic to each other.

***

Whatever may be our expectations from material awareness or spiritual awareness, it is the mind that is the powerhouse for both in order to experience and determine their impact. This is made possible only when we know how to conquer and control our own mind while it is transmitting thoughts. Thoughts too are a vibration of energy. When we think, this aware energy within vibrates, transmits and attracts what we wish to experience.

The power of the mind can be utilized to focus our thoughts on what we desire, and using them consciously with awareness is what enhances this power. It is thoughts that consume the maximum energy from our mind and have a direct influence on the results it can yield. The moment we gain a proper hold on our thoughts, we become the master of our mind and its infinite power. In this manner, we transcend from an ascent state of self-consciousness towards that ultimate unified state of oneness, defined as soul or divine consciousness.

***

We may think we know everything, but how many of us make a conscious effort to self-examine our own thought processes? How they move and what they demand? Also, why do we keep worrying due to insecurity in life? Irrespective of what we have (say, wealth and material comforts), why does life remain incomplete within us? Why is it that we are never content and why do we keep asking for more?

In order to alter or improve our condition, we first need to awaken our thoughts, thus making us self-aware. Thoughts flow the way water does, taking any route wherever it flows or the shape of the vessel in which it is contained. It requires a navigator to guide the thoughts in the right direction. The mind simply utilizes its power, accumulating and attaching itself to all that it can in self-interest, consciously or otherwise.

Instead of personally experiencing this power, most of us generally live on borrowed knowledge accumulated from various sources, allowing our thoughts to be influenced by others. We unconsciously listen to, follow and imitate, right from childhood, what we believe and who we look up to. These traits are what we need to self-analyse and self-experience, before we allow the mind to be convinced of the same.

***

We mostly allow the mind to remain directionless and surrender to circumstances in meek acceptance of what life provides us. In such cases, we may have a lot of knowledge but lack spiritual experience. Our ego remains shallow, gloating in self-esteem wherever it can or becoming angry, whenever someone else counters it with higher awareness. We should remember that the mind is our engine and we, through awareness, are its navigator.

The failure or success of the mind entirely depends upon how we steer its engine power. What we bring closer to its attention we will attract, not only from our own mind but also from the collective minds around us. Say, we focus our desire on money; spontaneously, we will devise creative methods by observing, experiencing and learning how to make more and more. We will attract forces all around to connect with our own, seeking that desire with greater intensity.

Therefore, we should be aware in which direction we wish to proceed: material or divine, what methods to apply and when to apply brakes. Our aware consciousness will guide our mind how to balance every moment. We should focus, with attention, on one thing at a time, creatively combining our energy with what we are conscious about. We then awaken to a new life with an abundance of power and full of opportunities.

***

We should be careful, as the mind is extremely smart and powerful; it will always try to outwit other minds, presuming it knows more and will also apply shortcuts to achieve its desired results. It relies mainly on external sensory organs to attain what it desires. If we wish to change, correct and improve ourselves and also be creative, we will have to experience, evoke and stir up our inner perceptions. If we don't, our mind is bound to lose control and go astray in pursuit of the mirage of desires. The attachments to those desires will lead us towards greed and will become the cause of anxiety and suffering.

In other words, our eyes, instead of seeing what is outside, will have to look inside; self-awareness should guide our mind as to what it should or should not do. The mind can only construct and transmit what we actually command it to do. It is this awareness within that handles the mind's power and consciousness controls the same. Say, while driving a car, it is the state or position of our awareness, which determines whether we know how to drive or not. However, it is consciousness, that quality of our awareness, which determines how well we can drive the vehicle.

Therefore, we should awaken to this truth and try to create our own destiny. Consciousness is that quality, which reflects what the mind perceives and conceives through awareness. It shows the calibre of what we are. Awareness is the state of our mind. It is a seeker, knower or doer, either awakened or ignorant. It acts through consciousness, which combines both and becomes the totality of our being.

***

It is the ignorant mind that unconsciously plants positive or negative thoughts in the subconscious mind. This data gets programmed by the intellect to later interpret and form what we call habits. If we consciously think and programme our minds with positive and good thoughts about life, the mind, out of habit, shall reproduce the same from the subconscious.

In this manner, the powers of our conscious and the subconscious mind collaborate for it to germinate what our inner self sows in it (i.e., in our mind). This is why we need to look inwards to observe and supervise what our busy mind is up to. We just cannot delegate that task to anyone else. Besides that, the inner self also synchronizes with other souls, subtly interacting and communicating with each other. Therefore, we should always remember the totality of life is not in its state of being (awareness) but more in its state of becoming (consciousness).

***

There is no such thing as luck or destiny; this is purely a man-made concept. If our mind displays and relays positive energy, it shall attract the same, inside out, the laws of nature will make us see only that side of others what we ourselves reflect. Meaning, if we think positively, we will see only positive traits in others. Such thinking will take us towards those people and circumstances with a positive attitude and a positive content, helping us to achieve what we want to.

***

The universe, as science explains, is one complete spectrum of energy, vibrating at different frequencies connected to each other in one continuum as a whole. Every action has a reaction, creating an impact on each other. Primarily due to its continuum, the universe responds as one whole unit. What we breathe – air – is in continuum with all other bodies; we are linked to each other, transferring and sharing life energy.

In other words, we are all interconnected, inter-related and interdependent on each other in one continuum. Our thoughts and intentions, which we emit to the surrounding energy, rebound and respond in the same manner in which they were emitted. Similarly, when we strongly focus upon any situation, we attract positivity by transmitting to the encircling energy, which, in turn, reciprocates by responding to whatever we visualize.

This is how we synchronize with external situations, which match with the images based in our own subconscious. Since we are the authors of this transmission, our personal psychic energy, we can make our circumstances (including coincidences) more meaningful. Say, if we are deeply focused on any subject, we attract outside forces connected to this subject to come to our aid. After that, we need to be attentive, alert and watchful to capture them as and when they come. We thus connect the outer with the inner to maximize the power of both our material and spiritual selves.

Chapter 4

How We See Ourselves

Searching all directions with one's awareness, one finds no one dearer than oneself. In the same way, others are fiercely dear to themselves. So, one should not hurt others if one loves oneself.

— Raja Sutta: The King*

We all know that appearances can be deceptive. How do we actually see ourselves? Does our public persona truly reflect what we are from within?

Ponder over this question. A person may look at a mirror and see only physical aspects such as the face, the chest, the arms and legs, but can he ever *truly see* the real self? In the mirror, a reflection is presented. This is a reflection of the light that hits the surface of the body. The image is reversed. It is not so easy to notice this aspect, unless some writing is held up to the mirror and then it becomes obvious that the letters are backwards. So what are we really seeing?

---

*An ancient Buddhist work, originally written in the Pali language.

When we engage with other people the same is true; we see only a reflection of ourselves, not necessarily our true selves. Other people may react to our physical appearance, personality, comments, or a combination of these, but do they actually know us, the real essence of who we are, our individuality? Not likely, because we do not reveal our inner self and also, in most cases, whether we agree or not, we do not even know our own self.

Our minds keep playing games, making us presume we know all. The reason is that we constantly change according to time, space and circumstance. Any perception of reality is only a momentary snapshot of that instant, taken by one particular conscious moment from one's own point of view. To be concise, it is fleeting, unreliable and not necessarily true.

We may profess that we do not care what others think of us. But our thoughts and actions will show otherwise. Every act, from dressing up to what we say and do or do not do, revolves around how best we can impress others, simply for the sake of maintaining our self-esteem. We all wish to be accepted and appreciated and will go to any extreme to hide our actuality, more to present a pleasing picture, so that we are not socially rejected. This may vary from one person to another in accordance to what ideas we have. Meaning, at the end of all this play, by claiming I am this and not that, basically, we all wish to be recognized as somebody.

***

Spiritually and scientifically, we all exist as one single constituent, emerging and going back into the same source called spirit or energy. Existentially, we are all unique. We all have a distinct personality, originating from the conditioning of our mental and physical characteristics. This personality provides us our individuality, depending on how we present ourselves during our lifetime to others and ourselves. Our personality may wither in time and space, but our individuality, which we create through our own uniqueness, remains eternal.

***

Our entire world or at least our concept of life is made up of perceptual 'snapshots' that are stitched together in a vast tapestry of human existence over time. We have made a model of reality and have created conditioned fields around it. On top of that, we expect our children to also see things the way we do. In such a conditioned field, an element of separation begins, where we consider ourselves as independent beings, within the whole or from that oneness in which we exist.

We mentally make a circle of our own, remaining within the periphery of 'me, mine and myself' comprising a cluster of thoughts, impressions and memories. We artificially define this collection in our minds as a conviction of how we see ourselves, giving it some form of meaning. We do not realize that life has a deeper meaning beyond 'our, me and mine', which can be discovered only when we remove such layers of conditioning and enter the core of the circle of our existence.

This is how we have created and separated our self and our family by creating artificial boundaries to separate one from another. The process collectively goes deeper in forming separate communities with their own defined religions, cultures, states and then nations. When the truth is that the entire earth is our home. We have created friends, families, dogmas and religions as a result of existing in that self-defined periphery.

The moment we establish any part of our consciousness as separate from the whole, we become attached to our self-identification. We then get surrounded by our ego, clinging to our likes and dislikes and continue to exist, conditioned within 'me, mine and myself'.

The key to a deeper understanding of the nature of reality is to question our concepts of it. Does anyone have the power to define reality and that too in a comprehensive way? Let us consider this analogy. If total perception represents a field from the floor to the ceiling, human perception is only a razor-thin slice of the total. This is very easy to prove: just make a list of the sounds that animals can hear and humans cannot. We must embrace our limitations and recognize them.

***

Scientific evidence, based on rational thoughts, has revealed that any onlooker's effect on the outcome of whatever is being observed is different for every person from its actual reality. It shows that the perceiver affects the perception. Further, our own ideas of what others think about us also hinge upon our own beliefs of who we are, because that is what we present to them. Our consciousness reflects what we think of this world and vice versa in the case of others.

***

Initially, we are shaped and groomed by our parents, especially by the mother. Then, friends, society and those whom we believe influence us. Most of us are, in fact, more of a product crafted and moulded by others, leaving aside a few who are rebels. They are the ones who create their own destiny by pro-acting with every call of natural instinct and the environment by their own personal power, irrespective of what has been told or dictated to them.

Therefore, all those we know are more of our own reflections; meaning if we are good, we will only see good in others. Similarly, if we think positive, we will not be able to notice the negativity of others. What we reflect from our consciousness is also more accessible to an outside observer, rather than ourselves. This is because our mind is always biased towards our own self. Eventually, even if we keep on presenting ourselves differently to others, inwardly our spiritual awareness, through integrity, intention and indulgence, shall determine who we really are.

It is also equally important to like ourselves. There are many who really do not like themselves or are not happy with their present circumstances. Comparisons, envy, demands, pressures and what not, bring down the faith in, and the impression of, one's self. We should remember that we have a strong relationship with our outer and inner selves. The simplest method for us is to spend some time in contemplation and enjoy that aloneness, in order to love our own company in solitude. It is only when we love our own selves that we shall be able to love others.

***

If we want to follow the Buddha's path of kindness and compassion, let us first bring out our own 'Buddhahood'. Let us see ourselves as truly sensitive to all that is around with love and compassion rather than being only concerned with self-interest. Transferring these traits on to others will create a ripple effect throughout the universe. Imagine that!

Chapter 5

THE PURPOSE OF LIFE

Life needs to be lived, experienced and realized – celebrated and enjoyed as it is, the way it is, demanding nothing from the past or the future but everything from the present.

— Gian Kumar

The meaning or purpose of life differs from one individual to another; some relate this factor to material satisfaction through desires, while others to pursuing spiritual freedom. Not only that, the meaning often changes from time to time with regard to one's age, gradual self-development and maturity. Some of us may consider our purpose in life is to appease God by going to a temple or other religious places and following rituals so that we can be rewarded by reaching heaven after death. There are others, who besides fulfilling their desires through the accumulation of wealth and material attachment, balance their life with spiritual development.

***

The debate over the meaning of life and death dates back to when the first humans walked this planet. For the common people, life is simply a person's biological existence between birth and death. However, scientists, spiritualists, academicians, philosophers and religious scholars have multiple views about this concept. If we start probing the mind seeking the spiritual meaning of human life, it demands only oneness in total freedom. Life needs to be celebrated and experienced every moment, righteously, by our own individuality, rather than be questioned on its purpose.

In spite of being the most elementary question of our existence, no one has been able to give a proper answer so far. Why are we here on this planet? This question itself may turn out to be meaningless because most of us are mainly concerned with the accumulation of wealth and material possessions for personal gratification rather than with humanity at large. However, I strongly believe life does have a deeper meaning.

The reason why nature has provided us with an extraordinary mind is to make life meaningful. The mind has given us all means to reveal its presence through our own uniqueness, which remains for eternity in the manner realized by exceptional individuals like the Buddha, Albert Einstein and many others. Therefore, we need to be first clear whether we are looking for that subjective meaning through spirituality or for those objective values, which the external world provides.

***

At some point or the other, all of us come to that crossroads where we begin questioning the meaning and purpose of life. Say, until the age of twenty, we are relatively innocent and carefree and not unduly concerned about life and its complexities; we simply enjoy every moment for what it is. Gradually, after that, ambition and responsibility 'invade', and desires and demands pervade, our lives. We keep trying to provide for our family and ourselves and constantly try to prove to the community who and what we are by amassing wealth and material assets. During this period, we are not much concerned about what is right or wrong; we are happy when we get what we want, otherwise not. We constantly strive to attain our goals, but continue brooding about the past or worrying about the future. We are objectively trying to achieve a certain goal in life.

***

Later, say, after crossing forty, we normally become wiser, introspect and contemplate whether all the accumulations and attachments that we keep clinging to justify the purpose of life. With age and time, most of us become mature, balanced and content, probably due to a decrease in our desires. We now wish to transform ourselves, learning from the mistakes of our past.

A serene sense of self-realization engulfs us, and we start on a journey of refinement in life. However, even then, many of us are still confused, with a gnawing feeling, about the real meaning or purpose of life. We may think that even this self-realization provides only a limited meaning, when we are subjectively concerned about the objective values in life.

We have no choice; the meaning of life is limited to the period that we exist. After we die, there is only nothingness. All that exists in this universe is nothing but absolute dark energy. We come from this dark energy and go back into the same. For a limited period we are granted consciousness, which makes us aware of all objects around. Therefore, the quality and quantity of life are restricted to its mortality and, sometimes, what we leave behind remains immortal.

***

In satisfying ourselves or, in proving to others how much we have achieved, acquired or attained will never give us that peace and joy, which we desire. Life will still remain incomplete; there will always be something amiss. This is when we realize that life is a not a goal but a journey. It is *living* with deep instinctive experiences that matters and we keep learning and practising the art of balancing health, wealth and wisdom. We learn the knack of giving without expectations, thereby understanding the reality about truth, love, faith, selflessness, detachment from worldly desires and so on.

There are ever so many subtle inner experiences, which are far more gratifying rather than proving to others by words and deeds, how great we are. To be alive, loving and smiling, and being joyful in all that we do, from one moment to the next, is simply living life to the full.

Let us compare from both perspectives, subjective and objective, what life has in store for us.

If we look at life subjectively, in the basic experience of how we live lies its meaning. It happens the moment we reduce our attachments connected to self-identification in 'me and mine'. The destruction of the ego is set into motion. We start looking, beyond our small selves, towards that larger picture of the oneness all around. This is how in the midst of that objective meaning of life, which purely exists in satiating our desires, a subjective realization enters.

***

Spiritually, if we can liberate our inner selves, not from desire but from that attachment to desire, we would know the true meaning of life. It is that attachment, which brings forth emotional reactions of happiness or sadness leading to disturbances in the vibrating energies of life. We go inwards from the ephemeral enjoyment of desires into the core of our inner being to discover the true purpose of life.

Objectively of course, we will notice that our world of ambitions and desires dictates life's purpose and meaning. We go on a rollercoaster ride adding one asset after another, accumulating, snatching and clinging to our possessions, and sometimes taking away from others all that we can, whatever be the cost.

It is said that, in spiritual existence, because of a higher degree of contentment, there is joy in every moment along with calm and peace. Death, as and when it comes, is accepted with grace since we would have lived our existence fully and are prepared to die at any time. The meaning of life and death transcends the body and mind and also those fancy words and attachments in searching for happiness. Anyone who has lived such a life in totality will never be afraid of death; its significance will be stressed more upon the completion and summing up of one's life. A life that is complete with material necessities *and* spiritual contentment.

***

Nature exists without any meaning; it just is, as it is, and we are a part of it. There is no purpose; it exists with pure intensity and totality. Life too is a part of nature; I would say do not spend too much time figuring out its meaning. The mind's job is to separate and choose between this and that, probing for a meaning to satisfy itself and, that too, objectively. We are required more to live with our bodily existence in consonance with nature selflessly, sensitively, spiritually and subjectively. The uniqueness within us will shine not by running after it or seeking some meaning, but by living and caring and experiencing every moment within that presence of ours in alert awareness.

***

Life is nothing but an experience to realize the paradoxical nature of existence. Subjectively, if we wish to know its purpose, there is only one: we should try to retain its spiritual presence as far as possible in its absoluteness, not allowing thoughts to separate everything into fragments. If we look within, we shall discover the spirit demanding a boundless unity. Objectively, yes, a strong meaning is definitely there, differing from one person to another; some would want to create an empire mainly to satisfy their desires. In both cases, nature has provided us with a mind, where we become the sole creator of our inner and outer worlds, either finding meaning in balance or in extremities.

***

Life, in fact, is a stage; we perform with an illusory existence in duality, relating through dichotomies. It is the mind that is creating those illusions and which is solely responsible for separating everything in order to choose and analyse in our self-interest. Our self-awareness becomes the navigator, overseeing this drama, experiencing this and that, and, consequently, summing everything up as our consciousness.

The illusion arises when our mind, out of ignorance, considers itself to be the real self, immersed in the ever-changing, impermanent nature of desires. When we spiritually understand, experience and realize who and what we really are, we become the architect of our mind and its destiny by acquiring the power of intuitive intelligence called spiritual awareness.

***

Therefore, if, at one end, there is ego with a shallow awareness, at the other end, we have a divine, intense awareness. This spiritual awareness is responsible for making the mind aware in order to become conscious, experience and realize the difference between the absolute and the dual characteristics of life. It also plays a part in centralizing both the separated forms of consciousness in their oneness in purity, where they actually belong.

***

Within and without, external and internal and with regard to the subject and the object, to begin with, acquiring knowledge is necessary. This knowledge is required in order to provide the correct direction for bringing separated realities in a balanced manner towards their centre. Both have the same absolute energy as their constituents. The ultimate purpose of a yogi (a spiritual experiencer) is to eradicate the difference between the two and experience oneness all around.

***

The purpose of life should be to live intuitively, where our presence should radiate certain uniqueness from our existence for all time to come. As mentioned in my book *The Ultimate Reality*,* we are not here to become saints or divine beings. Our purpose should be more towards

---

*Leadstart Publishing, Mumbai, 2015.

balancing those dualities, which relate to each other in paradoxes and in dichotomies.

***

We should make attempts to bring the dual factors of, say, positive and negative, closer towards their centre of oneness from their points of separation. It is for this purpose that the mind is designed to attain that goal in our self-interest. This can be done by surrendering our ego and accepting the dual factors, good or bad, with awareness and with equal grace. Only then can we lead a balanced life with joy in every moment, so that when death comes we accept it with grace in totality.

***

What is the best manner to live? We should balance our lifestyle, enjoying both the material and the spiritual existence in moderation. We should lead a life, in which there is something of everything: regular yogic exercises, correct food habits, devoting time to family and society, thinking and working for others and also for ourselves, reflecting upon ourselves in meditation, going with the flow and accepting happiness or sadness with grace.

***

We should live for the present and not fret about the past or the future. Normally, we notice that most of us are engrossed in some obsession or the other: money, sex, food or spiritualism. Such an obsession creates an imbalance causing a lot of stress, which depletes our energies, simply because other factors too demand our equal attention.

***

Humans, as a race, are blinded by ambition; our wants and desires seem unlimited. Most people spend 80 per cent of their lives craving for luxuries and pleasures for physical comfort. Such behaviour determines the extent of our ignorance vis-à-vis spiritualism. Further, religion, parents, friends, teachers and peers structure and condition our personalities. As a result of these rigid influences, we spend a lot of our energy devoting more time to imitating others in blind beliefs, entrapped by petty desires, losing that bigger picture of life.

At one end, if there are conditioned blind beliefs, then, at the other, we have our experiential knowledge. We need to think, analyse and be aware of the depth of realization of each end and its subsequent reality. What we need to do is to look within and experience and create our own individuality rather than a personality based upon imitating others' beliefs and lifestyles. We should question ourselves thus: Do we blindly believe and follow what our guru says or do we first analyse his words and then decide to follow the direction in which he directs us?

***

It requires courage to practise the faith we believe in, especially when it is created by our own free will. All we need are a caring heart, a conscious mind and a creative spirit. The key to achieving this objective is to acquire evolved experiential knowledge providing us that extra wisdom, which can never be attained by following others' experiences. We should always remember that what we are searching for is hidden within. We should lead our life by taking care of all three, body, mind and spirit, without fearing the inevitable, that is, death. Life is a precious gift; the purpose is to experience and realize every moment with everything in moderation, until the very end.

Chapter 6

SEEKING ENLIGHTENMENT

I truly attained nothing from complete, unexcelled Enlightenment.

— The Buddha

What is spiritual enlightenment? It means becoming aware of ourselves that we are not only the body and the mind but also the spirit. When all the three come close to their oneness, we experience and realize enlightenment. In other words, enlightenment is not something that we can attain as an object and hold on to. It is an entity that we can only realize out of experience, when the gross energy as the body and the subtle energy as the mind conjugate into one with the core as spirit.

The day we realize ourselves, our body and mind disappear; the spirit is illuminated in totality as one complete whole and, in such a state, we are considered as self-realized or God realized.

Enlightenment is difficult to describe in words because it is simply an experiential realization, without the person even coming to know that he is self-realized, since his mind can no longer create any distinctions in dualities.

Therefore, seeking spiritual enlightenment is simply a continuous process of transcending into a higher consciousness. It is not a trophy or something similar that you may attain. Enlightenment will only lead to confusion; it is neither a greater purpose in life nor a guarantee for being free from attachment and bondage. It does not change in any manner the reality within or without, whether we undertake physical, materialistic or mental renunciation. Those who run around seeking enlightenment in religion or spirituality with theoretical knowledge of mantras (sacred sounds), tantras (methods of attaining a higher awareness of consciousness) or yantras (geometric patterns) are only fooling themselves.

***

Enlightenment means raising our consciousness towards total awareness. It is more of a personal growth towards that ultimate realization: a vision of a goal. Seeking enlightenment, self-realization, pure consciousness, liberation, moksha (release from the cycle of birth and rebirth) or nirvana (a blissful or idyllic state) can happen only in theory.

Enlightenment is only meant for us to understand the ultimate: that life and physical existence become one and the same. Enlightenment refers not to being a part of God, but the ways and means of knowing, being, experiencing and realizing God Himself. Is this the purpose of our life or is it something else? Sages and spiritual masters refer to this as freedom, but freedom from what? Aren't we all here to also become a part of physical existence and to experience and realize both the good and the bad, the positive and the negative and God and the devil?

Without the presence of one, the other one would become meaningless. Can we fully eliminate and decimate one for the other? Only God can do so, but we are far from God realization and we should know that such imaginary projections in seeking this goal or that goal should not be based upon unfeasible realizations. We will find many self-proclaimed 'enlightened masters' adding prefixes before their names, without being self-realized with regard to absoluteness in body, mind or spirit, yet equating themselves to God. Yes! Followers also consider their gurus to be God-realized and there is nothing that will alter their faith, except their own experiential awareness.

The reason is that spiritual enlightenment is not something we can seek, for there is nothing to seek. Enlightenment, when considered objectively, is possible; in that state, we become more knowledgeable, mature and wise. In spirituality, enlightenment is more focused on freedom in liberating ourselves from all objective attachments and bonding. This spiritual freedom too is merely a metaphor; for as long as we exist, there is no freedom.

Let us take the example of a person who is taking his cow to sell in the market. He ties a rope around the cow's neck, and firmly holding this rope, freely walks, thinking about how much money he is going to make. He does not realize that neither he nor the cow is free, since both are bound with the same rope to each other until the cow is sold, ending that relationship altogether.

Similarly, so long as the soul is attached to the body and the mind, none of them is free. It is only death, which provides freedom, either through the disintegration of the body and the mind (which mingle with the earth) or through sadhana (dedicated spiritual practices) bringing both together into the soul as one. In both cases, death of the physical brain occurs and the body merges with the eternal, pure subjective soul.

***

People all over the world, who are in distress and depression, invariably go to gurus or preachers, seeking enlightenment. The dedicated presence of throngs in ashrams or similar institutions itself signifies the effort they have made in order to seek and learn about enlightenment. The guru or preacher, in return, through his hypnotic personality and power of oration, mesmerizes his followers. They soon go into a trance and, during that period, all their woes seem to come to an end. There is an infusion of fresh energy, temporarily making them forget their woes arising due to mental drudgery.

A blind belief engulfs them; they continue listening for days on end how to experience the ultimate in pure consciousness or God realization. How those 'artistes' running their spiritual businesses are going to enlighten millions of followers by the means and methods they provide is anybody's guess. The moment the masses distance themselves from a guru or a preacher, the big 'I' returns; the ego re-emerges and they are back in the same old rut, only worse than before.

Now, under the false pretence of being enlightened, they act as if they have been transported into a higher state of being. They repeat what has been taught to them and imitate their guru/s, fully convinced of this metamorphosis. They now develop a superiority complex and consider themselves to be in a higher realm, attempting to disseminate their new-found knowledge.

***

Even after a person has been awakened from his state of ignorance through self-knowledge about the illusions of physical existence and in spite of his knowing that he is not merely body and mind but also the awareness in the form of consciousness, he still fails to realize enlightenment. Intellectuality is not the recourse to enlightenment.

Why not? As mentioned earlier, enlightenment is not in its seeking, but is to be only experientially realized. In spiritual terms, knowledge brings more darkness; it remains only as past knowledge, enhancing our ego, influenced by others, until the same is practised, experienced and realized. Under this false illusion, an individual, after attaining knowledge, instead develops a delusion that he is enlightened.

Furthermore, by going to any guru or preacher, there is inconsequential transformation, until one self-experiences and realizes what one spiritually learns. This knowledge today can be acquired from various sources. Knowing of the ultimate reality, truth, love and transcendental meditation is of no help, unless self-experienced.

***

All enlightened factors are only experiences. Love, God and truth are pure experiences and their reality cannot be described objectively in words. Lord Krishna, the Buddha and Jesus Christ never knew that they were enlightened; it was their followers, who, much later, considered them to be self-realized. They were human beings like us, but with a higher consciousness. They experienced and realized their true nature with deeds of selflessness, compassion and sacrifice, spreading the message of oneness all around.

***

Therefore, in spirituality, we realize enlightenment only after we 'dissolve' the body and the mind into the spirit as one. There is no 'we' or 'us', and nothing but awareness of that selflessness exists. It is the spirit, which permeates, penetrates and prevails over all that is there as only one and not two in our universe.

The purpose of existence is not to seek God or become supernatural. In materialistic existence, we have to seek and fulfil desires and, in spiritual existence, we have to observe and witness, moment to moment, what the ego demands. Living and experiencing both forms of existence, in the right balance, make us complete. This is the purpose of life, where there is optimum realization of health, wealth and wisdom.

***

We are all a part of that same absolute constituent as God. But we normally exist in a state of separation, because of the mind being more inclined towards 'me, mine and myself'. Our purpose should be to live in totality, from one moment to the next, in mindfulness, to be aware, conscious and alive. Existence cannot be separate from us, since we are all interconnected, interdependent and inter-related as one whole. We all breathe the same air. Birth and death are merely entry and exit points, and, during the interim period, our objective should be to enjoy both the material and spiritual worlds.

The purpose of existence should not be to seek or desire the incomprehensible; such seeking or desiring is related to the future. The experience of the divine and that of life are in the present. The mind is nothing but ego and, through external cognitive thinking, it is designed only for the past and the future. It is the desire to achieve or acquire something in the future that becomes the fundamental cause of our anxiety and suffering. What we need to do is to *spiritually experience* the power of this moment with awareness. Connecting all the three, the past, the present and the future, results in a journey of life in totality.

***

It is only religion that preaches or implies that we are here in this world for some greater or divine purpose. Since this idea or theory has been embedded in our mind for generations and we have been conditioned to accept it, many people, including those from the West who come to India, seek enlightenment through spiritualism. When they do not attain what they seek, they feel dejected and disappointed. At the risk of sounding repetitive, let me state that the purpose, aim or intention in life is not to seek or desire enlightenment. For instance, the Buddha never knew he was enlightened; yet he went on to realize greatness.

There comes a point in our life when seeking anything ends; we have no choice but to act, experience and realize. We then come to the realization that we already have what we have been seeking. What we require is awareness in the form of light to dispel the darkness within. Awareness is nothing but light energy, permeating the mind to enlighten us and to get rid of all our ignorance. Enlightenment is merely the explosion of knowledge to make us understand and realize our own selves.

***

Reality asserts: 'I am in "the now"; I exist in the now and also have to be experienced in the now. I am that absolute, changing from dust to life and back into dust.' Therefore, the salvation or the evolution that we seek in the future can only be had *in the present*. It is to be experienced in totality, moment to moment, with alertness, watchfulness and awareness, when godliness in selflessness flows naturally, not with any purpose, but because of our being alert and aware.

The message of religion should be to unite everyone with belief in one God and to live each moment joyously in totality. Religion today unfortunately, gives us separate identities. Consequently, we lose connections and communication with each other as also compassion for fellow human beings.

***

Enlightenment reveals who and what we already are and is present within us as the subtle witnessing self; there is nothing to seek, only to awaken and realize. What we really need to do is to live in balance, with totality, amongst family, friends and others, taking care to balance all three: mind, body and soul. This can be made possible not by seeking desires with self-interest, but by a selfless attitude full of compassion and by the surrender of the ego.

The fundamental rule in spirituality claims: 'I am that,' meaning we are already enlightened. We always remain as the *witnessing self* in the absolute presence of that awareness, with the mind and the body doing the experiencing. When the experiencer (with the self as the subject) experiencing (through mind) becomes the experienced (the object/situation at hand), we realize enlightenment.

We then become the subject in totality with all as one and what remains after that is nothing, but the source as pure light. We are like a sage, also called a 'seer', the one who sees all with this energy of life called 'light'. This 'seeing' itself, without any thoughts or ideas, leads to total freedom from all bondages.

Chapter 7

THREE TECHNIQUES OF MEDITATION

Mindfulness is a quality that's always there. It's an illusion that there's a meditation and post-meditation period, because you're either mindful or you're not.

— Richard Gere*

Meditation today is considered a panacea for all the stresses of modern-day living. It has even found its way into the corporate world, where it is believed to enhance productivity of the employees. In reality, it is a state of discipline, where we detach our mind to reach a stage of alertness with awareness, without thinking. When the consciousness of any person detaches itself from the objects that the mind perceives, this state is referred to as 'thoughtless or choiceless awareness'.

The history of meditation and yoga goes back over 5000 years, and many references can be found in ancient Indian scriptures. The earliest archaeological records stem from the Vedic tradition in India. Tantric meditation, as performed by Lord Shiva goes back even further, which

*Richard Gere (born 31 August 1949) is a renowned Hollywood actor and a humanitarian activist.

later, around 500 BCE, became an integral part of many other religious texts in different parts of the world.

***

Whether we are beginners or long-term meditators and whether we meditate to decrease stress or to become intuitively aware, the benefits of meditation are enormous. Scientific research has shown that meditation does the following:

- It improves our physical as well as mental health;
- it sharpens our skills and lowers our anxiety levels; and
- it controls our blood pressure and improves our overall immunity.

Scientific, yogic and personal benefits today provide enough motivation for us to consider meditation seriously as a daily activity.

***

There are three basic types of meditation, all exploring consciousness in different manners.

The first is to focus attention on any one chosen subject by going inwards, away from our chattering thoughts. It is like cleansing the mind of all the stress and anxiety, as a daily routine, so that the mind is refreshed and relaxed.

The second type involves the submerging of our mind in deep concentration through chanting mantras and carrying out various methods of breathing for a specific and well-defined reason.

The third type is living in meditation, a stage of mindfulness from one moment to the next, in thoughtless awareness. It is auto-transcending, where no effort or thinking is applied; indulgence is in pure observation with alert watchfulness, along with the presence of spontaneous awareness.

***

In the first type, which can be termed transcendental meditation (TM) and which is similar to Raja Yoga, is a form of exercise that aims to take control over the mind and the emotions in a state of relaxed awareness. Yoga, besides meditation, also incorporates diet, exercise, breathing and relaxation as its primary features. TM is very popular in many parts of the world, though not with the same name, but with the same techniques and is a part of the Vedic custom in India. Maharishi Mahesh Yogi (1918 to 2008), a revolutionary leader in the world of yoga, was the founder of TM. It is generally taught by certified teachers and is practised for around thirty minutes a day, in a relaxed posture with closed eyes.

We come to the second type: mantra meditation. Chanting actually is a different practice when compared to meditation, since the former is related to sound and the latter to silence. Both serve the same purpose: to relax the mind with awareness. Each has some advantages over the other. Chanting of mantras overrides certain limitations of meditation as we can recite these mantras at any place or time in any posture. In order to enhance our practice of meditation, chanting of mantras comes as a valuable tool. What we need to remember is chanting should not be mechanical; the repetition of the words or lines, in order to have its effect, should be done with full awareness. It is also important that we should know the meaning of the mantra and there should be some feeling behind the whole exercise.

***

'Aum (or Om) Namah Shivaya' is the prime mantra, meaning: 'I bow to Shiva.' It is a chant related to the unified consciousness of the universe and is the mantra for meditation. Mantras that we chant are basically sounds, syllables or words that radiate intense sound energy. They initially originated from the Vedas and japa-mantras are highly suitable for meditation containing seed letters with strong vibrating energy and having a subtle meaning.

Mantra, tantra, yoga and mindfulness are all linked to one fundamental ingredient: awareness, either spontaneously or through effort. All the four combine with awareness to form meditation. Meditation means awareness and mindfulness, in turn, means the effortless awareness to be in the present, moment to moment, with every experience. Every concept originates from the mind and it is awareness that gives rise to everything that the mind has ever perceived or conceived. Awareness is the spiritual source of the mind from which the mind functions and relates to the external world.

***

In the third type, i.e., meditation with mindfulness, we do not concentrate or contemplate and nor do we practise these activities; they simply need to become part of our basic nature. When thoughts subside, meditation begins. When we just watch our mind, without thinking, with observance and alertness, we become aware. We become a witness to our own mind, watching and witnessing. Meditation, with such awareness, takes us deeply into the subject. We feel the luminous awareness of the self. Meditation takes us away from 'me and mine' and from our desirous self, to what we really are, existentially in silence, where there are no words, language, logic or reasoning, reminding us that we are not our physical identity, name, religion or nationality, but consciousness in continuity.

***

Actual meditation is not for five, ten or fifteen minutes, like in transcendental meditation, which is more of a therapy. The true objective of meditation is to get away from the past and the future to live in the present, from one moment to the next. We should be awake, alert, observant and aware in order to express our spontaneity. A sage is also called a *seer* because he does not *do* anything; he simply *sees*. When we see with awareness, we as the subject, become one with the object and know it, but when we think, we separate the two trying to figure out the details. Meditation in this case is to live in the spontaneous now, without any interference from thoughts of duality. It is the process of centring our energies towards that oneness to which we belong.

***

Spiritual awareness differs from the ordinary, since it makes our mind aware of our own thoughts, feelings and actions, other than being generally aware of the outer world. It fundamentally points towards any present moment with complete consciousness. Hence we are considered to be spiritual only when we are aware of our inner presence and how mindfully our presence of awareness exhibits itself.

Furthermore, in spiritual awareness, watching and witnessing from moment to moment is the key factor. We should not think or be identified with any object, for that would base us entirely upon the past and the future. Witnessing the mind from this inner spirit in choiceless thoughts, while interacting with the outer world, is the ultimate mantra of all spiritual techniques.

***

Commonly, many consider meditation as a means for mental relaxation, whereas, in spirituality, it is just the opposite. It claims that once we become aware and conscious, our proactive attitude in spontaneity, followed by our actions, is bound to automatically relax our mind.

The mind is phenomenal and thoughts are all that we have to communicate with our inner self and outer self. However, thoughts are highly prejudiced, primarily in our self-interest, inviting trouble and also becoming uncontrollable. There is simply no space or silence between any two thoughts. Spirituality provides us the answer with that technique in mindfulness: how to make our mind relax on its own, effortlessly.

According to spirituality, when the mind is chattering incessantly, we should just watch: we will become aware and the mind, on its own, will become still. The past and the future worlds will disappear and we will enter the realm of thoughtlessness in choiceless awareness, purely in the present. We will, without any intention, create that space of silence, where there are no words or language to explain, justify or choose, but only the presence of our aware energy simply watching and witnessing in the now.

When in deep sleep, the mind is unconscious and not aware. However, when the mind is awake and witnessing, at that moment, there are no thoughts and this allows all three, our body, mind and spirit, to conjoin in meditative awareness. Therefore, we should not condemn or appreciate. We should not attach ourselves to any of our desires or emotions. We should remain inclusive, with every subject as one, without allowing thoughts to separate everything into this or that. The past will disappear and neither will we be anxious about the future. What will appear is only the present, existentially in every moment for us to celebrate and enjoy.

The mind is attuned to thinking of the past and the future, taking us away from the present. Mindfulness plugs this gap and connects all three: the past, the present and the future. The mind behaves in a reactive state to all that is happening in the present; mindfulness brings us into a proactive mode of action, non-judgementally. In mindfulness there are no emotions involved; we simply respond to any stimulus with equanimity and with alert awareness.

Chapter 8

THE NEED FOR A GURU

You have to grow from the inside out. None can teach you, none can make you spiritual. There is no other teacher but your own soul.

— Swami Vivekananda

Sometime back, I gave my opinion in the media negating the need for a guru; most of the reactions, as expected, were against my beliefs and thoughts on this subject. Since this is a delicate issue, kindly allow me to elaborate.

There is no denying the fact that the word 'guru' is a very esteemed and venerated one, more to be worshipped than merely respected; the guru is the source for removing our ignorance, awakening our soul and guiding it towards God. Translated from Sanskrit, 'gu' stands for spiritual ignorance and 'ru' for that luminous knowledge of the spirit that dispels ignorance. We all know that, in spiritualism, the role of a guru is essential, from teaching yoga to tantra to acquiring knowledge and wisdom.

***

The basic difference between a teacher and a guru is that the former will educate us about the outside and the guru is supposed to take us inwards. A teacher will develop our intellect, whereas a guru will make us *realize* that intellect. A teacher is qualified in what he teaches, whereas a guru needs to be experientially realized on what he preaches. Most people believe that a guru can dispel the darkness surrounding us, which results from desires and material accumulations and attachments.

***

What exactly are the qualities and qualifications, which justify such a lofty position for a guru?

A guru, with all his spiritual knowledge, should be experienced in what he teaches and should be worthy enough to impart to the shishyas (disciples or students) the profundity and significance of the sacred scriptures of India's glorious heritage. A guru needs to be highly selective in accepting students; he should choose those who are serious, devoted and responsive to spiritual transmission in actual practice and not merely brag about the subject.

When both these conditions are favourable, only then can a guru and student dissolve into one. A guru needs to be self-aware and self-realized and also should not be carried away by the illusory existence of our materialistic world. He should not project his name, photos, promotional campaigns and so on for acquiring fame for himself or his institution. During the ancient period, when gurus played a major and dominant role in society, a lot of students would seek self-realization to serve humankind. In the bygone days, most people did not have books or the Internet in order to attain knowledge about their inner world and inner reality. Today, apart from the guru, we have many other means of attaining spiritual knowledge, which awakens us and leads us into knowing who and what we are and who is God.

Presently, there are certain renowned gurus who themselves have categorically denounced the need for a guru. In fact, a real guru, if asked the question whether or not a guru is necessary, will reply that there is no such need. A guru's entire role is mainly to point out to the disciple, which direction he or she needs to follow. The anecdotes that follow exemplify what I am trying to express.

***

According to an ancient Indian scripture:

> Fools dwelling in darkness, wise in their own conceit, and puffed up with vain knowledge, go round and round staggering to and fro, like blind men led by the blind (Katha Upanishad, I, ii, 5).

The world today is full of such fools. Almost everyone wants to be a guru and disseminate 'knowledge and spirituality'– through ashrams, books, TV or the Internet – hoping to make a fast buck in the process.

As Swami Vivekananda declared: 'Everyone wants to be a teacher; every beggar wants to make a gift of a million dollars! Just as these beggars are ridiculous, so are these teachers.'

***

The great Swami Ramakrishna Paramahamsa* had always maintained that the true guru is within each one of us. He himself was self-realized and without a guru.

---

*Ramakrishna Paramahamsa (18 February 1836 to 16 August 1886; real name Gadadhar Chattopadhyay) was an Indian mystic and yogi. His chief disciple was Swami Vivekananda.

The true guru is innate, functioning as our witnessing self and residing within us as the formless pure consciousness. What we need to do is to awaken to this truth. No one can help us be ourselves, especially when the job of any guru is primarily to teach us how to know our own self. That is what spirituality is all about: to live graciously with our inner spirit, awakened to a reality of how to be in the presence of who we are.

A guru, I repeat, though necessary at the initial stages of our life, need not necessarily be in human form; we can receive the same knowledge from books or other sources. When we understand from this knowledge that we are not just the body and the mind, but the spirit, we begin to realize ourselves. The guru, whom we were searching for outside, appears from within to guide us from then onwards towards God. Both the guru and the self become one and the same.

***

Many of us who are in a state of distress, depression, anxiety or those who are mentally weak, may require the presence of a physical guru.

According to a well-known story, once ten men had to cross a river. They swam across and the leader, after reaching the other bank, started counting. As per his estimate, only nine men were there. He evidently forgot to count himself. The leader kept on counting again and again but could not discover the tenth man as he forgot to include himself each time he counted. He did not realize that mere knowledge of counting and seeking through blind action was not going to reveal the tenth man. In such a situation, a teacher with experience is needed to point out that he, as the leader, is the tenth man.

***

The world of materialism is so very captivating and powerful that our desires in material attachments to feeling insecure make us want more and more, mainly out of greed and fear. As a result, we tend to accumulate wealth and other status-enhancing items (such as expensive cars or opulent mansions) and develop attachments to them, inviting anxiety, suffering and sorrow, especially if there is a loss of status. Agreed, some medium is definitely required to guide us and to disclose to us and point to us the right direction to pursue in life, but this knowledge can be attained today from various sources, when we are more independent to agree or disagree.

If we become aware that we are supposed to expand our mental horizons, evolve with the passage of time and not get emotionally attached to our possessions, the real transformation begins. Ambition provides that fundamental energy for us to grow and expand. However, with our third eye open (as a result of inner awareness), we can experience and realize with humaneness and humility the oneness of the mind, the body and the spirit. This is what spiritualism is all about.

***

When the guru dissolves in the shishya in total bhakti (devotion), this is an enlightening experience. A guru is that person who is self-realized enough to impart sankhya (knowledge of the self) to make us realize we are the embodiment of awareness, which by itself is actionless, changeless, timeless, spaceless and limitless.

***

Spiritual energy, after manifesting itself in the mind, makes us aware and conscious and we realize that both the material world and the spiritual world are essential for existence. A guru's job is not only to provide higher knowledge on this subject but also to direct us how to transcend this material stage and move towards contentment, peace and joy. Such gurus are definitely in short supply today.

***

Since childhood we are virtually being dictated to how to think, eat, live and behave by our parents, relatives, teachers, peers and other community members. So much so that, in many cases, our future too is planned as per our parents' wishes. This is why we notice that most of us are conditioned, dependent and weak, requiring a pillar to lean on. Our individuality gets impaired and, lacking confidence, we are ready to follow anybody just on the basis of hearsay that so-and-so guru is great. There is a lack of inner reasoning within our common sense, which, being the most significant part of our intellect, goes haywire. We go in pursuit of mirages, remaining ignorant of not being able to understand, experience and realize who we really are.

***

It needs to be remembered that consciousness can exist only in the self and can manifest itself in the mind through awareness gained by experience. This consciousness develops our inner ability, creating our individuality: that uniqueness comprising what we are. We should not lose or waste this individuality in proving to others that we are somebody else and not who we really are. We are that wonderful self; we ought to realize, with awareness of this simple *'is-ness'*, the quality of our own presence.

No one can help us to be our own selves; we have to do so ourselves. If we are unable to do so and still need help, we need to find a *real* guru, who will help us in making us aware of what we have forgotten and centralize our energies in restoring us to what we really were (and are).

This is what real meditation is: to be able to live from one moment to the next in awareness, for which we really need no one but ourselves. Most gurus of today can only relate to us their own experiences. Moreover, a common person today faces a lot of difficulty in directly approaching and interacting with a guru. In the Vedanta times, gurus were realized beings and had fewer disciples compared to the hundreds of thousands of followers that virtually each enterprising guru has today.

***

First, what I have noticed over the years is that some people visit a guru with the hope and belief that they would be granted whatever they desire, which probably they feel God has denied them.

Secondly, I have come across others visiting gurus out of fear for all the misdeeds they have done; for example, politicians and wealthy businessmen to absolve themselves from their wrongdoings. Weak-minded and depressed people rush to gurus in the hope of finding and filling up what they are missing in life.

***

Nowadays, ashrams and similar institutions require huge funds to maintain their ever-growing size and clientele. (Some of them have come to resemble five-star hotels!) In such a situation, a guru is left with no other option but to market himself, making efforts that demand, from his followers, loyalty, devotion, time and money. Eventually, all these factors, when combined, result in more of a business proposition rather than the purpose for which they were meant.

Gurus in the ancient times were very much different; the purpose of teaching was to convert a student into a master. But today, the intention is to increase the number of blind followers in the hope of making more and more money. Such followers remain in their dream world, ignorant of the realities, and continue to sing paeans of how great their gurus are. In such a scenario, instead of practising those spiritual methods to experience and realize the essence of their gurus' teachings, most disciples indulge in gossip (as a result of their ego consciousness) and boast about their knowledge of the subject using obscure and abstruse Sanskrit terminology.

Instead of falling into the trap of money-minded gurus, we should wake up and understand the ground realities, kindle the spirit within us, and comprehend that we are everything that God wishes us to be; we just need to experience and realize that. We need to open our minds to the fact that gurus are neither extraordinary nor supernatural. We are simply swayed as their blind devotees into believing they are incarnations of God in the form of avatars.

What we see today is a spiritual mask trying to conceal the flourishing businesses of various gurus in the guise of providing joy and contentment. Spiritual teachers play their role as brand ambassadors for particular schools of thought. In actuality, a majority of their followers are simple, common people who come with faith, blindly following the teachings of the gurus in the hope of obtaining relief from their grief, despair or agony or trying to make both ends meet.

***

The present-day spiritual gurus ostensibly seek to take their followers to extreme levels of enlightenment on how to recognize the ultimate teachings about pure consciousness, soul, atman (the spiritual life principle of the universe), God realization and so on. The gurus know very well that, under normal circumstances, it is just not possible to achieve this objective. The result is that, in blind belief, the followers keep on clinging to the same guru/s in the hope of receiving salvation, one day or the other.

One may well ask: What good has the aforementioned sort of spiritualism, religion or the love for an external God done so far, except to increase substantially the number of followers? In fact, at present, we fear God more than we love Him. We can probably count on our fingers the number of followers who have attained enlightenment from their gurus' teachings. This is true for both religion and spiritualism; both have failed to make much of an impact. Most of the self-proclaimed gurus, with fancy prefixes attached to their names, provide only temporary relief to their followers from their sufferings. Also, it shocks us when we come across media reports that exploiting spiritualism to the hilt is one of the easiest avenues of acquiring wealth, besides selling drugs and weapons!

The crucial question arises: why do people run after such so-called spiritual gurus? Today as I see it, world-famous gurus have millions of followers. As a result of their brilliant personalities and superb eloquence, they are providing immediate relief to those who are desperate and in despair. But the priorities of most of the gurus are the rich and the powerful, who flock to them in large numbers. Please tell me where do I stand as a common man in such a long queue? Until and unless I can convince my guru that I am a worthy servant ready to perform all sorts of services for his empire, I stand no chance of getting closer to him.

Therefore, before we make any attempts to visit a guru or even think of following one, it is imperative that we first self-enquire on our motive for doing so. Are we so weak that we need to seek outside help? Are we so ignorant that we should follow a herd seeking a supernatural phenomenon?

Under normal circumstances, from our own daily experiences of ethics and morality, if we seriously contemplate on them, that should be more than enough to guide us on the right path. Mother Nature responds to those who seek in earnest from their own inner self that what we are seeking, we already are.

***

The subject of spiritualism is complex and the experience to realize the self is difficult and seemingly never-ending. In their quest for spiritual salvation, seekers travel here and there looking for that source, which can provide the right direction. As mentioned earlier, in their ignorance, they do not seem to realize that the destination, which they seek, is inside and not outside.

The answer lies not in spiritualism but in spirituality. The former is only a theory and the latter is its practice. The mind in a state of awareness plays a primary role in realizing what we wish on the basis of proper self-experience. Therefore, we should follow the methods of yoga and practise meditation instead of running here and there, wasting time, money and energy. We can learn quite a lot from the Internet and from books. We are bound to transcend the self if we practise sincerely; after that, we will truthfully declare to our own conscience as to how spiritual we are.

***

The crux of the ancient epic Mahabharata revolves around the teachings of Lord Krishna (an avatar of Lord Vishnu) given to the expert archer Arjuna (also called Partha) in the Bhagvadgita. Krishna, also known as Parthasarathy (Partha's charioteer), was more of a friend to Arjuna and not a guru.

Therefore, we should not be dependent on anybody (including a guru), who can take away our sense of individuality. In the garb of enforcing discipline, he is bound to make us abide by his own ego, experiences and whims. If we need to surrender to someone it should be to ourselves; but, before that, we should get rid of our own inflated ego. Surrendering to a guru will only make us vulnerable, susceptive and reactive (and not proactive).

***

The highly respected sage, Ramana Maharishi (30 December 1879 to 14 April 1950), rightly opined that a guru need not necessarily be in human form; according to him, a guru is that source, which conveys that 'God is within you. Dive within and realize. God, Guru and the Self are the same'.

Chapter 9

WHAT IS REALITY?

We are all different expressions of one reality, different songs of one singer, different dances of one dancer, different paintings – but the painter is one.

— Osho*

The interpretation of reality has changed over time. Until the early nineteenth century, the pre-modern theory prevailed, which stated that 'objective reality exists and is revealed by divine intervention'. Later, modern theory propounded during the twentieth century specified that 'objective truth does exist but it is based on rationality and structured order'. Post-modernity considers objective truth more subjectively, based upon each person's observation and experience. Whatever we perceive is first filtered and then dealt with according to our thoughts and beliefs. Essentially, on the whole, from all the data that is collected through our senses, the mind constructs a meaningful view of our environment and calls it real.

---

*Osho, also known as Rajneesh (born as Chandra Mohan Jain: 11 December 1931 to 19 January 1990), was viewed as a mystic guru and a spiritual teacher.

How do we establish whether *our reality is actually real*? The definitions of reality differ with respect to science, spirituality and religion. So, are we permitted to consider the nature of reality to be whatever we feel it is? What we observe, know and experience intellectually may be our own reality, differing from others' versions. No two human minds can perceive identical realities. Therefore, it is difficult to assign a clear definition to reality, unless we measure the same, which is impossible. What we see in front of us may be real, but it is our mind, which decides what we actually *perceive*. The mind filters what is of interest from the stream of data that pours in every moment and considers it to be real.

***

The Hindus have a term, 'maya' (illusion), for such an apparent reality, where things seem to be real or true but are not necessarily so. Reality today is determined by each individual's mind and not by its actuality. One scientist may consider something to be real, knowing very well that another is bound to contradict the same. Reality in the material world is a dualistic product of the individual conscious mind. It will continue to be so, as long as the collective mind or society agrees with it.

Absolute reality is like the sky: changeless, limitless, spaceless and infinite. It is independent of one's mind. In religion, it is considered a personal God; science considers it to be energy and spirituality the impersonal spirit. However, in such interpretations, they all represent and reflect the same ingredient, the absolute. It is the reality of all realities. It exists as the absolute energy and has two aspects: transcendent and inherent. Through its supreme power called 'maya', the absolute gets manifested inherently within the mind in time and space to exist and also to experience and realize the dualities and dichotomies of life.

***

The reality present in our mind is, in fact, a delusion, dealing in opposites, differing from one moment to another. One needs to eliminate the mind from the senses to understand what reality is in its absolute form. The human mind is bound to use its intellect to discern and quantify what it sees. In absolute terms, reality is just the way it exists in the now, as it is. If we tell someone 'you are beautiful', it has no meaning in absolute terms. Beauty is in the eyes of the beholder, so that again is one person's reality. The world we experience through our mind is nothing but a waking experience of what our senses observe. These experiences, which are only apparent, manifest themselves within the mind. They do not necessarily represent the actual quality or absoluteness of the situation.

Therefore, when the mind is ignorant, we should awaken it and make it knowledgeable. When it wanders to the past and the future, we should bring it back to the present. And when it is chattering, we should hush it. However, when the mind is intuitive, we should allow ideas and thoughts to come, because reality can only be grasped, not with imagination, but with intuitive and spontaneous awareness. Awareness is that reality, which cannot be comprehended with our mind dealing in opposites; for that we have the intellect to choose and discern between this and that. What we need is to be alert and watchful to capture this reality. In our existence with duality, though part of the absolute but separated, we see images of both real and unreal. In actuality, only the real can exist; the other follows like a shadow. Happiness is our nature, which is real, but our desires and demands suppress our true nature, bringing in sadness and despair.

***

According to the Vedanta philosophy of ancient India, the images, which the mind constructs, are more of an illusion. The absolute and the infinite Brahman (the ultimate reality), from which everything emerges and into which everything dissolves, is the fundamental truth of life. What is manifested in the mind is constantly changing; but in reality all that exists is one changeless absolute spirit, energy or Brahman. The absolute manifests itself in many different forms, thereby deluding the mind from its actuality and creating all sorts of desires and greed through ego consciousness.

Primordial consciousness from our experiences creates a relative reality. Even though our consciousness will always determine the nature of our reality, we cannot ignore the fact that it is limited to physical reality, which by itself is the cause of all our illusions.

Actual reality has its own independent character and existence, which do not depend on any of the mind's apprehensions. The mind's perception can only allow and assist us in knowing any entity in relation to its opposite. We should keep in mind that absolute reality is the ultimate fabric of our universe; the more we probe through the mind, the harder it becomes to comprehend. The experiences of our separated identity in egocentricity, or our singular vision of this world, are nothing but a psychic phenomenon of our mind.

***

It is our spiritual awareness, which brings us closer to our reality. The higher the inner spiritual quotient, the more intense will be the level of experiential consciousness that we will realize. Creation is one, both of the spiritual and the material. It is only after experiencing both that we become wise enough to realize this absolute reality of oneness in all that exists. In the spiritual realm, matter is not relevant, but the form that matter assumes, is.

***

Knowing the difference between the relative and absolute realities gives us a wider perspective about the nature of our own self. We need to raise the level of our consciousness to the extent where we should not be deluded that our daily experiences are the foundation of reality. We tend to get attached to the same, causing anxiety and suffering. We must realize the message dictated by the ultimate that we are all interrelated and interdependent as one single reality. Unless there is a feeling of oneness, inner peace and tranquillity will not prevail.

Since the realm of reality is refracted through our limited senses, we are not able to see or observe the actual reality. It gets restricted to what *appears* to be real. Nevertheless, the Brahman is real, the world is real and we are real, but we do not seem to experience the same directly. We simply see only the body and the mind to be real; however that is impermanent, since the underlying reality resides within as the eternal spirit.

***

There is also no such thing as unreal; only *one* entity exists. It is the mind, which separates the one entity into its relative components to compare and experience its own personal reality. When we see an object with naked eyes, the reality says it is 'X'. When we see the same object, through a microscope, the reality becomes 'Y'. If we penetrate deeper, through a more powerful gadget, it may become 'Z'.

Hence, we need to awaken to the fact that besides the body and the mind, we also need to experience our inner reality. All have to be taken in unison as one composite unit and not in their separation. Both the Brahman and the world (physical) are real, the former in its changeless actuality and the latter being its interchangeable attribute; both need to be seen as one and not two.

Then what is it that is really real? We need to keep in mind that the universe exists only because we are aware of it. We are aware of not only what we observe outside but also our own inner self. This tells us that the outside is the total reality but our mind separates that into fragments to observe its individual perceptive reality.

Therefore, the resultant of our subjective (in totality), objective (separated by mind) and individual realities are three different aspects of the one and same aware energy, which permits us to perceive all three.

Science comprehends the outer reality of the universe in its quantum level, which are packets of energy in interchangeable forms within an infinite entity as one whole. The inner reality in its individual experiential quality has been referred to as 'qualia'. *Therefore, actual reality is nothing but aware energy, which makes us also aware of being aware and originates from within a microcosm leading us towards that macrocosm, where all that exists is only real.*

Chapter 10

ENJOYING LIFE: SLOW AND STEADY

There is more to life than increasing its speed.

— Mahatma Gandhi

The time we have at our disposal in today's world is finite and precious. I am sure we will all agree that it must be used resourcefully and judiciously.

It is by doing so that we have been able to reach the jet age and develop the Internet and our digital world where speed is considered to be of prime importance. The intention is to provide us with more quality time to do other things. However, the paradox is that we always have less time, but more amenities and gizmos. There are so many things we wish to do, but time is always short. Therefore, we are always in a hurry; speed is required in everything we do from eating to praying to fulfilling our constant and limitless desires.

***

Let us first consider what time and space are all about. The sages, from the ancient days, have been claiming that space and time are curved like a circle and not flat. Meaning the surface of the earth and also the periphery of motion in the vibration of any form of energy are in a circular and cyclical manner. Spinning like a wheel, this energy exists in this spaceless, timeless universe moving in a vortex, whether inside our body in the form of chakras (wheels) or seasons according to the movement of our planets.

***

However, the mind, in order to capture the duration of a situation in any restricted space of what it observes, relates to that in a linear sense of past, present and future. Meaning we can only observe motions capacitated to a limited space of what we experience during that duration. This concept of observation is measured by the mind mathematically as the distance between any two points of what we experience and call time.

I repeat: without the mind there would be no independent existence of either space or time. Actual reality consists of only the present moment. We can only watch a movement in space and measure that duration in a specified time–space relationship, which is purely a mathematical representation. Say, if we throw a stone in the air, it only moves in space; the distance between any two points (in the stone's trajectory) becomes our past, present and future dividing that into units of time taken.

However, our consciousness requires a particular moment to consider what it observes, experiences and realizes to get things done in the relative world. The mind simultaneously also has the capacity to witness any movement of psychic energy from one moment to the next, in order to make it aware of every stage of happening events. These moments of our presence in consciousness differ from one individual to another.

***

In space, what exists is only now; the mathematical calculation of time is devised by the mind only for its own convenience. Psychologically, the duration or time taken to evaluate any situation differs from one person to another, depending on how one experiences that moment. Therefore, the chronological time and the psychological time in any experience of any moment differ from each other.

We can experience the needles of our watch moving in space in a circular pattern, besides what they reveal through numerical measurement. Consciousness also has the capability to be aware, watch and witness this numerical order, called time. Time is a scientific phenomenon and consciousness a spiritual one, both merge into one.

Let us now probe spiritually this aspect of the space–time relationship.

During our lifetime, we are constantly in a hurry to get things done within the limited space and time available to us. Today, youngsters in their thirties are falling victim to anxiety and depression besides contracting diseases related to stress such as hypertension.

In order to save time, our lives are moving too fast and also becoming complex and cluttered due to multitasking. We have no choice but to ask, either due to compulsion or through common sense, is this really worth it?

***

What actually is it, that we want from life and is there any purpose to our lives? At such moments, a subject that we thought was never meant for us starts making sense and we become conscious of its significance. Our consciousness is now disciplined to understand and experience life: how to use our mind like an instrument and not be used by it.

When we are young, we feel that we have absolutely no time to waste; it is very precious and we have lots to do and miles to go before we can sleep. We all have high expectations and are ambitiously driven by the ego, zooming towards acquiring more and more. Our mind keeps dictating how, what, when and where it wishes to achieve its objectives in the rat race unleashed by our space–time relationship.

A stage comes when we realize the stupidity of running only after name, fame and money at the cost of our health, peace of mind and integrity. We begin to question whether material acquisition is all that life has to offer? We pick up books, browse the Internet or look for other sources to enquire and ascertain how we can start all over again, on a higher platform to achieve peace of mind and joyful contentment, which is more satisfying than just competing with, and feeling jealous of, our peers and becoming obsessed with wanting more and more. We now begin the process of self-examination and discover the true meaning and purpose of life.

We soon, spiritually, reach that crossroads between the material and the spiritual, amid limited space and time with both entities having their own respective relevance. This is the most crucial junction in our lives and, at this moment, we need the right guidance and the right source to direct us on this new journey to discover our true self. It is a journey of the inner self, where we become less calculating and more meditative.

***

The real self, that ingredient residing within us, witnessing all that we do, makes our mind think, experience and realize the unpredictability of life. No technology, digitization or science can come to our aid, when we wish to know our real self, beyond the functioning of our cognitive mind. We eventually realize that the mind is actually our instrument to observe, monitor, navigate and control in the manner that we wish. And we are the presence of that core energy subsumed in awareness covered by layers of gross energy as the body and subtle energy in the form of the mind.

***

As mentioned in the epigraph to this chapter, Mahatma Gandhi once said: 'There is more to life than increasing its speed.' Therefore, we need to slow down the pace of our thoughts, speech and activities and reduce the seemingly crazy speed in which we are moving every day and note the difference. Such a change in lifestyle will take us beyond the ego and ambition into a new dimension of life, where we can now learn more about our consciousness. Very few of us, only those who are serious seekers, manage to capture the correct connection in understanding the transmutation of the soul from ego consciousness to the realm of the divine.

First, we have to learn how to be alert and observant in the present moment. We need to breathe slowly, meditate and calm ourselves and keep away from the daily barrage of stresses, tensions and anxieties. We have to practise how to surrender our mind and accept any situation with grace the way it is, good or bad. Our thoughts will be still, but the mind will be dynamic and focused in the present moment. Less time will be wasted in brooding about the past and the future.

***

Second, we should spend more time in listening, rather than being in a hurry to interrupt others and force them to accept our point of view. We need to forget about the watch and the calendar and enjoy the beauty of nature as manifested by the sky, stars, mountains, rivers and landscapes. We should try and relax even in a busy street café or in a bustling mall and see how everyone else seems to be in a hurry.

***

One should read this chapter – in, fact, the entire book – slowly and ponder over its content. One will discover that one can absorb and assimilate much more when one reads a little and contemplates, rather than going through everything in a hurry.

***

There are some people who may not wish to get involved in such a serious study and practice of the methods of spirituality. For them, we can provide other options if they wish to slow down their 'fast and furious' lifestyles.

Almost all over the world, resorts have opened up with diverse surroundings comprising spas and rejuvenating centres to epitomize a slow-paced and fulfilling holiday.

Such resorts offer various facilities (such as health clubs, gyms and swimming pools) and are usually located on beaches or mountains amidst a beautiful, natural environment and fabulous landscapes, taking us away from the hustle and bustle of cities.

Admittedly, such getaways are but temporary; we need to decide, one day or the other, whether we are seeking temporary relief or we are searching for long-lasting joy and contentment in peace and tranquillity.

The answer, of course, lies in finding the right balance between the two options. An existence comprising both the material and the spiritual is vital and necessary. In the material world, time and speed are essential to advance, grow and fly high. The balance is achieved, only when we bring in its opposite, the spiritual, to transcend from one to the other, where we shine with wisdom in both realms.

***

Fulfilment in the journey of life is realized when, through sincere efforts and hard work, we first attain wealth and material comforts, acquire what we desire, and after we are content, we go beyond the material world towards that higher spiritual realm where we really belong.

In this state, consciousness expands and we realize the benefits of being sensitive to all aspects of our existence. The real purpose of life can be found in such a totality, where there is comfort, joy and peace in everything.

Life should always be treated as a journey that seeks its natural path rather than fixing too many goals. Life should move from quantity towards quality, with both the body and the mind being under our control. We should not be governed by the clock and must find enough time for our family, our friends and ourselves.

***

I found the contents of this chapter making a lot of sense. As a result, I have toned down my feverish pitch and now enjoy what I do. In my case, I am doing what I really wished (and wish) to do: indulge in my passion for writing. I find this activity to be meditative; it helps me focus on the present moment with a sense of awareness. Writing has made my life all the more worthwhile.

***

As life goes by, unconsciously, we keep brooding, multitasking, worrying and trying to achieve more and more. Technology keeps advancing, revealing to us how to extract more from nature and time. Before we can enjoy what we have achieved, the list of demands keeps on increasing and the time for fulfilling them keeps on decreasing. We finally break down and wonder what life is really all about.

Life, in fact, is more about monotasking rather than doing a multitude of things at the same time. It demands our consciousness and awareness to appreciate every little experience. It requires the presence of our being in that very moment, rather than our mind going at different tangents. When we are alert, aware and focused, our presence gets dynamically involved from moment to moment, in 'the now'. Life connects our past and future to the present. Whether it is cleaning our toilet or listening to our favourite music, we are involved in totality.

In this chapter, slowing down is used as a metaphor; we need to be mindful of what we do. Mindfulness involves the presence of our being there from one moment to the next in totality. Despite the fact that we cannot survive in today's world without the mobile phone or the computer, even then we should stop using them for a while to enjoy the peace and tranquillity provided by the other aspects of life. If business meetings, marketing strategies and making money are imperative, so is connecting and spending quality time with our immediate family, other relatives and friends and in natural surroundings.

***

Today, our minds and bodies pull in different directions; the body may be physically present with our partner, but our mind may be elsewhere. We (meaning city dwellers) spend more time in offices, cars and malls, forgetting the beauty of life and the abundance of nature. We should learn how to enjoy what we have in hand rather than looking at others, comparing ourselves with them and wanting more and more. We should not rely on the mind and the time taken in our activities, but instead feel the presence of spiritual awareness in whatever we do in completeness.

We should stop constantly checking our mobile phones, e-mail, Facebook and Twitter. We need to learn how to regulate our activities properly and lead a life in totality with quality and not with quantity. This learning process itself is akin to meditation, with the constant presence of our awareness in what we do.

We need not be perfectionists in all our activities; we should not overburden the mind with our obsessions. A relaxed but watchful approach at times can be more productive and effortless than applying extra energy to force the results to come out the way we want. I repeat: *we should always remember that life is a journey not a goal.*

The problems in life start with comparison. We keep on imitating or copying what others (mainly affluent celebrities) do, trying to be what we are not. It is like a sickness. We are all unique and howsoever hard we may try, we can never be that somebody who appeals to us. So, we should be original, content and happy with small as well as big things in life.

Chapter 11

SPIRITUAL BUT NOT RELIGIOUS

We have just enough religion to make us hate, but not enough to make us love one another.

— Jonathan Swift*

Nowadays, *being spiritual* has become a popular phrase to signify those who *do not accept* traditional organized religion in furthering their inner growth. Spiritual but not religious (SBNR) today is mostly prominent in the United States of America, where, as per one survey, around 25 per cent of the population identifies more with SBNR than any other demographic region in the world. The term is gaining popularity with evolving new-age spiritualism, where the reference to God is more towards a higher power or transcendent nature of reality, having no connection with any religious affiliation.

***

The oldest form of spiritualism, still being practised today, originated in India. Over 5000 years ago, sages in India imparted their spiritual wisdom in a complex form

---

*Jonathan Swift (1667 to 1745) was an Anglo-Irish writer and satirist. His most famous work is *Gulliver's Travels* (1726).

of ancient Sanskrit language to a specialized section of society. In order to make their wise teachings simpler to understand, they were narrated to the masses in the form of stories and fables. Some esoteric people, making full use of their specialized knowledge and on the basis of their own interpretations, converted the contents of these narratives into blind (but strong) beliefs, leading to superstitions and irrational thinking. After that, they developed rituals, customs, doctrines and, finally, religion.

***

India, despite all its spiritual wisdom, today, is a muddle of religions, castes, creeds, dogmas, superstitions and traditions. Hinduism – one of the world's oldest known religions, but without any single founder and without a set of common teachings – is still practised by millions of people in India and elsewhere. Spiritualism is gradually losing its own originality and getting mixed with religion, with blind beliefs turning into intense faith. Self-discovery/self-development today is based more upon religious dogmas rather than the methods of experiencing how to develop spiritual awareness. Numerous gurus influence large numbers of followers referring to either subject as and when convenient, synonymously using both spirituality and religion.

Religion entails a set of organized practices based upon specific beliefs, cultures, ceremonies and traditions. Spirituality is a composite process involving yoga, meditation and tantra to unite the body, the mind and the spirit as one. It is based entirely upon one's personal experiences in search of a higher consciousness, which may or may not coincide with the tenets of religion/s.

Therefore, what we have today is the philosophy of spirituality diverging in three distinct directions. The first goes towards religion, the second towards beliefs in past life, regression, the continuity of the soul after death, pure consciousness, atman (the spiritual life principle of the universe) and God realization. The third is confined to simple methods of spirituality to develop a higher state of awareness in that absoluteness of who, what and how we are.

***

Over a period of time, religion has encompassed spiritualism to such an extent that it has become very difficult to explain to those who are weak-minded, dependent on others or rigid with blind beliefs the distinctions among the above three divergent views. However, the basic difference will always remain; organized religion separates one human being from another into Hindu, Muslim, Sikh or Christian, whereas spiritualism unites all in oneness with the doctrine of the spirit being its one and only reality.

Religion, in fact, has been embedded in our genes over centuries of conditioning. Our subconscious is tuned to think of a personal God, more out of fear and anxiety rather than on the basis of love and happiness. Spirituality, on the other hand, is in-built into an individual's basic character that makes him rise above materialism, caste or creed and comprehend the deeper dimensions of life. Spirituality is so very inclusive that, in order to become spiritual, we need not disregard or give up any religion. We simply transcend into a higher state of consciousness where there is grace and love for all religions and their tenets and practices. In fact, we become religious without following any particular religion.

***

The mind has been conditioned to such an extent that even an atheist, in spite of claiming a disbelief in religion, is confused. Religion has been so strong over the centuries that it has compelled even non-believers to inadvertently support the creed or sect (including its culture and ceremonies) they have been born into and in which their community believes. Since the time politics and religion have come together, it has become difficult not to voice support for our own contender/s.

However, conceptually, both religion and spirituality have the same foundation. To live in harmony with one and all, we must develop a respect for nature and be aware of our spiritual potential to reveal the inherent divinity within all of us. In practice, religion and spirituality seem to differ in their approach towards the meaning and purpose of life.

***

Those who are clear in their mind vis-à-vis SBNR reject any traditional organized religion as one of the basic formats to further their spiritual growth. Their main aim is to experience spirituality as a journey to discover who and what they are in order to attain self-realization despite the paradoxes and illusions of a materialistic existence.

Spirituality comes into focus when we ponder on the co-existence of our lives with the cosmic concurrence that we are all interdependent, inter-related and interconnected to each other. We delve deeper into the subject to understand the relevance behind the reason why we are here. Awareness in spirituality is that essence of life within which we are to celebrate all aspects of existence consciously. It is an in-depth experience making us aware of that inner truth lying dormant within. It makes us understand what the mind is all about, drawing us closer towards the universal spirit as one.

Spiritually, each one of us is potentially divine. In order to awaken this divinity, we need to go in for meditation with mindfulness. In this state, our thoughts are still but the mind is active, alert and observant. Meditation is the route, universal love is the essence and selfless service is the ultimate feature of this journey towards oneness. Its basic principle revolves around the pivot that we are all a single absolute unified energy in continuum. This fundamental energy manifests itself in different forms, each with its own respective attributes, which keep varying, but on its own remains changeless.

***

Religions have their own separate forms of divinity from doctrines to dogmas, from scriptures to statuettes and from temples to testaments. Eventually, in theory, they are supposed to finally merge into the same oneness, but do not in reality. Religion, if we are not aware, becomes a very personal matter, which can arouse intense emotions and may lead to hatred in one human being towards another.

In religion, we do not seem to care what is right or wrong with regard to any religious issue. We simply hold a belief, which turns into deep faith and we are totally convinced that our religious sentiments and precepts are superior to others'. We, along with our ego, are ready to go to battle over this issue.

Belief, as we know, is neither experiential nor existential and does not lay any stress on knowing the truth. It is simply conditioned and downloaded into our subconscious mind, which we all follow. It invariably defies logic and commonsense, enhancing our psychic rigidity.

Organized religion, though meant for spreading love, compassion and peace, seldom serves a higher purpose when it comes to understanding the inner truth. When any religion with a separate personal God organizes a set of people or a community to move towards its teachings and rituals, whatever be the message, it is bound to be separatist and divisive. Droves of people are driven to religion out of fear and insecurity and it is sad that such a beautiful concept has turned into a breeding ground for war and terror, instead of promoting love and unity.

***

Spirituality, on the other hand, emerges the moment one feels the oneness within as a result of a deeper inner power. A certain meaning to our existence emerges and becomes a process for experiencing life so very differently from religion. One wonders how these two have become synonymous to each other. Even though religion was designed to practise methods provided by spirituality, however, the moment it got organized by separate communities, it simply overpowered everything and took control over humankind. Religion preaches about the existence of God; spirituality makes us experience and realize that God is present in our acts of godliness.

***

In conclusion, yes, I can honestly say I do practise spirituality. Initially coming from a staunch religious family, I did follow certain norms of religion for the sake of my elders and, later, I did so more out of fear and want. As soon as I became independent, I listened to my inner self. I started treading on that spiritual path, where my prayers are with respect to deities of all religions. All personal Gods to me are higher incarnations of the same consciousness that I am a part of. Today, when I pray, it makes me feel that I am in the presence of those divine souls, drawing, from their higher consciousness, an inspiration for creating a unified world.

Chapter 12

THE POWER OF LANGUAGE

Because of language, man has access to the past and the future. He can express the true and the untrue. Language helps him understand both what is and what could be.

— Wesley Douglass Camp*

What we speak emerges from the primary force of our intellect. Even though we may think in words, the very same words, when conveyed in the form of language, have the power to limit or set us free, frighten us or evoke courage in us, based upon our sensory perceptions. It's what we say that makes us who we are. In order to live well, the usage of right words at the right time becomes necessary to have control over, or to achieve balance in, any situation.

***

When someone speaks, we do not know whether those thoughts, which are later converted into speech,

---

*Wesley Douglass Camp (1915 to 1991), Preface to *What a Piece of Work Is Man: Camp's Unfamiliar Quotations from 2000 B.C. to the Present*, Prentice-Hall, New Jersey, USA, 1989.

are intuitive or emerging from an analytical mind. In whatever way, if and when we communicate well, it does wonders. Normally, we respond and react to internal and external stimuli as per the time, the situation and the circumstances, reflecting our character built up on the basis of our past experiences in life. However, when we speak, we try to regulate our words with the right intonation in the right quantum at the right time and the right place. We also seek to express certain emotions in words, hoping that others will understand and appreciate them.

There are times when we try to convey our feelings using the minimum number of words; at other times, we do not even say anything, hoping that our eyes, facial expressions and body language would do the 'talking'. However, we also have to be careful to control our impulsive outbursts. This situation is much in contrast to otherwise trying to prove why we are correct in any situation by speaking aloud. The wounds inflicted by words are far more damaging and difficult to heal rather than those caused by any other means (say, by physical assault).

There are also times when we tend to speak more than we should or speak rudely or in an arrogant manner, which we later regret. We should always be aware and conscious of what we speak. Once spoken, words cannot be taken back and the consequences have to be faced, whether good or bad.

***

We often remark: 'Speech is silver; silence is golden.' Silence dominates over speech on various occasions; it is also common to find that people who know more speak less. For instance, a good painter will let his work speak on his behalf. There are moments when we realize that more than saying the right thing at the right time, it is better to leave unsaid the wrong thing at the wrong time. On the other hand, the power of speech coming out directly from our intellect has the ability to influence any situation, pleasant or otherwise. A case to validate this point: most politicians generally can debate for or against any situation and are able to convince others to accept their viewpoints.

However, if we are following the path of self-discovery and inner development, the deeper we comprehend ourselves through self-examination, the calmer and quieter we become. We perceive and experience, while being alert and attentive, watching everything with awareness. As a result, we become more of listeners than talkers. The deeper we enter this field of spiritual silence, the more aloneness and solitude become our companions. Intuitiveness and spontaneous intelligence take over the intellect, when the present moment is all that we care for by not brooding over thoughts and words related to the past or the future.

***

Today, modulating ourselves to say the right things at the right times has made us artificial. Eventually, it is the soundness and the strength of our character and not speech that reflect our personality. However, we should also keep in mind that in a state of silence, the mind has this tendency to isolate us from any conversation. I feel that we should not hesitate to speak, if and when any situation demands, where, by saying a few words we express what we really wish to, so that we don't regret our silence later. What is required is that right balance between speech and silence; in the manner in which any two sounds are separated by gaps of silence.

***

The power of language is so strong that it is important we choose our words carefully. If we observe our vocabulary and the pattern of our language, we will come to know what we really are. For example, if there was fear or uncertainty within us, we would use words/terms such as '*I cannot*', '*I could have*' and '*I would have*'. This trend means that we are in a negative phase. We can also change ourselves by changing the usage of our words. Say, when referring to any mistake we may have made, we should tell ourselves that it has been more of a learning experience rather than an admittance of doing something wrong. In this manner, we can change our whole outlook towards that error.

Language is but an interpretation of duality, describing everything and every event in relative terms in order to define them. We are required to think and express our thoughts and ideas by going into the past, projecting them into the future, using our intellect and performing our karmas purely in self-interest. A human being, in order to communicate with himself and with others, requires language; it is a necessity. Through our words, we create our world. Life acquires meaning only when we know how to describe it.

***

Spiritually, language is a hindrance for human beings. It is based more upon living proactively, watching attentively and acting in spontaneity with awareness rather than emotionally reacting with thoughts in words. Here, language or thoughts in words are a barrier. No other living creature, in order to exist, requires a language to speak; for instance, animals do not use language as we know it, but have their own means of communication through a wide range of sounds.

It is only human society, which is built upon language, where worldly affairs are an outgrowth of language. At times, our life patterns give rise to anxiety, worry, depression and suffering. Such a condition makes us live for tomorrow, seeking something in the future, missing 'the now' because the mind is caught up in thoughts, ideas and words.

In the material world language is essential; however, in the spiritual realm what we need is peace of mind by watching everything with alertness and awareness in order to experience without thinking. We have to live existentially; i.e., spontaneously from one moment to the next. Solitude, silence and meditation with mindfulness are vital and obligatory. Therefore, for a materialistic mind to connect with the community, religion, society and culture, the medium of language is necessary.

In spiritual terms, for the soul or consciousness to expand and rise, watchfulness with awareness in silence is the answer. Both (watchfulness and awareness) are necessary as they are inseparable. In the material world, we must connect with language, but existentially, we must connect in silence with sensitivity, warmth and love to all with aware consciousness.

We should remember that a commune is necessary, whether we are in a physical or spiritual state, since we are all interconnected and inter-related. The members of the commune may be connected through silence, telepathy or language. A commune is required for the transfer of collective energy to set things in motion. We have to make our presence felt to each other. It may be in any form: through silence, words, gestures or other means. The fellowship in togetherness needs to continue. Nevertheless, the separated energies existing in duality will keep trying to unite and connect and this process will go on until they become one in total silence as the ultimate communion.

Chapter 13

THE PURSUIT OF SILENCE

The purpose of yoga is to silence your body, mind and soul so that all three can effortlessly unite into one.

— Gian Kumar

'Speech is silver; silence is golden' runs the adage. If speech is great, silence is greater. Let us imagine that we are sitting quietly amidst nature (say, in an orchard), surrounded by its lush beauty, and we awaken just as twilight breaks through. The scenario is marked by serenity and quietness. We wish that the inner peace and tranquillity bestowed by this scenario should remain forever. In this present day and age, when noise and chaos are inevitably prevalent in most urban areas across the world, we will come across very few places, which are soundless, unless artificially created in a confined space. Speech, as we know, is restricted to external space and time, but silence is connected to that space within us, which is as vast and deep as eternity.

***

Silence is pure splendour and absolute. For it is sound that is dual; it needs a source to be transmitted and a receiver to hear its transmission. Between any two notes of a sound, there is a gap of silence, which *defines* that sound. Sound, on further expansion, is expressed through words and language, which also belong to the dual category.

Silence is the source within which sound is its field. Sound does not possess the property of absorption. It keeps getting detached from its centre and moves into a higher or lower pitch, losing its identity until it reaches back into silence, where again it begins with a new note. Whenever we are disturbed, we will notice silence drawing closer to us. It is silence, which ultimately encompasses sound and brings about unity and oneness.

***

Silence, quietude or stillness makes us realize who we really are. We should silence the mind and make it quiet; this act breaks the chain of thoughts. At that moment, we enter a state of contemplation or start going inwards away from all the restless chattering of thoughts, the blaring of the TV, the beeping of mobile phones and so on.

***

Learning how to make our minds remain still or travel inwards is the latest exercise these days; it is the modern anti-anxiety medicine. From New York to New Delhi, the techniques and practices for acquiring inner peace has become big business. In this lucrative field, systems such as vaastu,* fengshui** and Reiki (the Japanese art of healing), apart from new-age gurus, astrologers,

---

*An ancient Indian science of architecture in harmony with nature.
**A Chinese philosophical system of harmonizing all human beings with the environment.

psychiatrists, psychologists and yoga teachers, are all attempting to teach ways and means of making the mind stay still. They guide us from designing buildings (vaastu) to meditation to gentle stretching and from chanting mantras while sitting in a quiet candle-lit room to breathing exercises and to the intricacies of yoga.

***

The fact is that, today, we are all in a hurry. Our ambitions and desires are driving us mad, bringing turmoil into our lives because they are mainly driven by greed and fear. Greed tells us there is no time to lose, whereas fear says we may lose our possessions, so we should cling on to them. In this manner, we undergo daily pressures that make our life complex in trying to accumulate too much in too short a time, eventually breaking down physically, emotionally and mentally, while being restless and ill.

Life, in fact, has now become one big noise. Living is noisy and demanding. It is only when we are tired, dejected or defeated that we become silent, for we cannot live totally in a silent environment. Silence is an art of wisdom; it teaches us how to have control over our thoughts. It also allows us to value the inward aspects of life.

***

When we observe silence, we move closer to that inner space within our body and mind. The mind is highly dynamic and communicates inwardly when there is a presence of awareness in the 'sound of silence'. It means that, spiritually, sound has more of an essence while experiencing it rather than in its words and meaning. We connect with that sound through complete concentration in awareness to become one with it.

In the hustle and bustle of city life, excess noise and hectic activity are almost omnipresent. Our mind gets tuned to a psychic extravaganza of random thoughts converging towards emotional desires in self-interest. When we silence those thoughts, we experience intense awareness in a poised manner and also tranquillity; we reach that meditative zone where there is no noise but pure melody.

***

Quietude is the beginning of the journey towards inner freedom or inner peace. In fact, meditation involves complete stillness of the mind. Through stillness, we quieten our thoughts, but the mind still remains active in order to indulge spontaneously in the present moment. It need not waver or brood over thoughts of the past and the future. In this state, we become intensely aware of the nature of our being. The mind tells us that we should not keep on hurrying in our lives despite rapid advances in technology and digitalization through multitasking. We should instead be able to focus, with a silent but more alive mind, increasingly, on monotasking. Then we can probably achieve greater results.

If we notice carefully, everything happens in the universe silently and peacefully without any contradictions. For instance, the solar system functions exquisitely, sending out the message that things happen in nature *in spite of* us and not *because of* us. In the same manner, in order to exist, sound, words, language, thoughts and the mind may have brought us to where we are today, but without silence, the story of life is never complete. Therefore to create a perfect symphony, we must use both silence and sound appropriately for the sake of harmony and not for discord in our lives.

***

Since our physical world is so very different from our inner being, we need to make space for both. We need to get away from this perpetual hegemony of sound that surrounds us. Spiritually, silence is referred to as that immeasurable space inside, or the inner sanctuary, where God dwells. From prayer to meditation, the mind requires silence, both inner and outer, to connect with the spirit to know 'who' we really are. When there is silence within, it indicates that we are not perturbed inside despite the incessant chattering of our mind. In such a state, even if we are in a noisy environment, there is a serene comfort for us to enjoy at that moment.

In silence can be discovered the beauty found in the diversity of landscapes: from mountains to beaches and from deserts to jungles. Such beauty is so overwhelming that no words are required to describe it. Silence is existential; it occurs in 'the now'. Without our knowing, all things happen in quietness, whether in creation, destruction or re-creation. It is through words that we later try to explain our experiences, in our self-interest, referring and relating them to opposites, whether good or bad.

In spirituality, we can communicate far more through silence, being one with the surroundings, than through words.

***

Silence in worldly terms may refer to the absence of noise, but, spiritually, silence is the source of sound and the nature of any sound is its meditative aspect.

In a spiritual ambience, silence does not mean the absence of sound; it means the beginning of seeing and listening within ourselves. It is that spiritual connect to one focal sound, when we experience a particular sound, be it a chant or a mantra or music. There is less of hearing and more of our being in the presence of that sound.

***

The mind is the link between the objective world and us. Only in the wakeful state is our mind conscious and our sensory organs interact with the material world. The mind cannot stop thinking; the more we try, the worse the situation becomes. We may halt our thinking faculties for a little while, but that would be counter-productive.

Silence or stillness, unless in deep sleep, needs to be alive, active and constructive. We need to witness, watch and feel with alertness in silence. We may be in the midst of a noisy market, but if we are alert and watchful, with the least amount of thoughts in our mind, the presence of our being will be mindful and complete.

If we practise to silence our mind by getting rid of thoughts and feelings and by not judging this person or that person, our ego becomes quiet. We then speak less about ourselves and do not force our opinions on others; not do we denigrate or try to control others. We become a witness to our own mind and also experience and realize the tranquillity within in a poised manner.

***

Silence facilitates our inner search by simply reducing the constant chattering of the mind. It brings us closer to the presence of our being, to reality, to truth and to the essence of our real self. The mind, through its thoughts, does just the opposite. It transports us to a separate world of our own, where language is used more for the accumulation of wealth and material attachments and also for the sake of fulfilling our desires, physical or otherwise, apart from gaining identities of our own (say, as celebrities in different fields).

***

If loneliness expresses the agony of silence, then solitude does just the opposite. We become sensitive to our inner aloneness. Both solitude and aloneness increase our awareness, making us more conscious of our actions. In such a state, the outside world cannot easily disturb us or disrupt our lives.

***

Words may come and go, but silence will remain forever. We may find silence in a church or a temple, but that would be an escape from reality. The real silence should be found in the environment in which we exist, with inner stillness, which awakens our being conjoined as a substratum of all that exists. Intellectually, we may hear sounds and separate them through language into their duality, but silence is existential; it can only be watched, observed and understood.

***

Life, reality, love, truth and silence are all experiences in subjectivity and we try to define them by words in objectivity. The moment we put them into words, the whole essence gets distorted and different interpretations are given. For example, truth, when experienced in silence, retains its absolute nature, but when explained by words, it changes into duality because it gets related to its dichotomy in lies. These forces will remain undefeated, because they are beyond us, and act as bridges to connect the subjective world to the objective world. Therefore, silence is a powerful declaration; those who can perceive us in silence will know more of who we are.

Chapter 14

THE MIND AND ITS AWARENESS

The ultimate value of life depends upon awareness and the power of contemplation rather than upon mere survival.

— Aristotle*

Awareness is of paramount importance in spirituality. In fact, spirituality emphasizes that the awareness of our presence is because of the presence of that awareness. In other words, awareness reveals who we really are. The determination of the existence of awareness also requires awareness. Allow me to explain in detail the meaning behind this complex statement. The mind is determined by the *state* of our awareness and consciousness is decided by the *quality* of our awareness. Awareness is that core energy over which there is a layer of subtle energy in the form of the mind and a layer of gross energy in the form of the body.

***

Since the mind is activated by awareness, it becomes the sole benefactor of 'who we are' and is responsible for

---

*Aristotle (384–322 B.C.) was an ancient Greek philosopher, scientist and teacher.

formulating our consciousness, which further determines 'what we are'. This 'maxim' encompasses the whole subject of spirituality, including its meaning. It tries to impart a certain message, which we normally ignore. It subtly conveys whether we are asleep, awake or dreaming that 'I am that awareness', which is always alive.

Spirituality seeks to dispel our ignorance about existing in duality, which revolves unconsciously in a vicious cycle of pleasure and pain. It also enlightens us about the illusory world of desires, cautioning us not to fall victim to temporary sensuous pleasures by considering them to be the ultimate source of happiness. It makes us journey beyond the material world into a spiritual realm, where we are in command of our body, mind and spirit as one.

***

Spiritual awareness means different things to different people. In fact, very few of us are able to understand what it indicates and designates. Science is still in a nascent stage with respect to understanding the function of awareness and its linkage with consciousness. It is only after we become aware that we are conscious. It is not our mental or physical being, but our inner spiritual presence, which expands and evolves our consciousness and guides it towards the divine or the devil. It is that consciousness, which due to its quality of awareness is everything to us; it is from this consciousness that we recognize and realize everything from the subatomic particle to the vastness of the universe.

***

The mind is the most miraculous machine created by nature, empowering us to perceive clearly and imbibe fully all that we observe in our unique personal world. What we observe becomes our reality.

Raw energy, after manifesting itself in the mind, activates and makes it alive. Awareness remains independent, because of its non-dual characteristics. It oversees all that the mind experiences, making it aware and capable of forming our individual consciousness. Awareness behaves as the witnessing self in its primordial stage and bridges the gap between the mind and its consciousness. The wider the gap, the less is the awareness and the more the gap, the more is the ego consciousness in us. The higher the awareness, we consciously lessen the gap between the spiritual and the material and move towards divine consciousness. If the mind is what drives our body to be in sync with the environment, awareness is the energy that makes our mind to be in sync through the oneness that we are in with the universe.

***

In simple terms, let me start with this premise. The moment we consider the mind and body as parts that belong to us, it indicates we are not independent of these two entities. Otherwise, we would not be saying 'our' mind says this or that. Further, we have the capacity and ability to observe, read, navigate and govern our own mind. If we consider ourselves as distinct and different from our minds, the question arises: WHO are we?

It is only through awareness that we can take care of our body and mind. It is that energy created by awareness, which makes our mind become conscious in order to experience and realize life. This series of experiences that the mind goes through, in turn, becomes our memory, forming the content of what we are, which is also referred to as consciousness.

Today, science has come to accept that matter – from the subatomic particles to the universe – represents only energy in different forms, which can be neither created nor destroyed, and always remains constant.

Spiritualism, on the other hand, from the prehistoric times, has always declared that the absolute spirit is what reigns supreme and all that exists in this universe is unified and not separate.

Spiritualism, as a theory, is generally misinterpreted; many have started relating it with God, religion and mysticism, accusing it of leading to regression by raking up our past life as well as the philosophy of an afterlife. It elaborates on the continuity of consciousness to pass from one life to the next.

The practice of spiritualism, which is spirituality, simply means how to be aware, mindful and conscious. And all we require for that is to be aware, watchful, attentive and authentic.

Therefore, when energy manifests itself and suffuses the mind, it originates as awareness, similar to how breathing keeps our body alive and kicking; awareness does that to our mind.

Whether we sleep, awake or dream, the mind in, all the three stages, is comprised of different levels of the intelligence-manifested energy called awareness. All creation in this world by human beings has been accredited to awareness. It creates our existence and then allows consciousness to take over. The higher the intensity, the greater is the absorption by the mind.

***

Plain and simple, awareness is that source, which determines our aliveness, allowing our mind to create its own existence. It is the state of our mind whose quality is determined by our consciousness. This entity, in turn, exists by attaching itself to experiencing life in dual living, relating to opposites.

When we are fast asleep, our mind becomes unconscious, the sense organs become inactive, the body is resting and everything slows down, but not our awareness. The moment someone nudges us, awareness, which never sleeps, spontaneously brings us back into action and we realize who and what we are. It is only after death that there is absence of awareness. The difference among our dreams, sleep or wakefulness is in the level of awareness; but so long as we are alive, awareness remains active. We should try and go to sleep with a question in our mind and, while we are asleep, the awareness within shall have an answer ready for us when we awaken.

***

Awareness is the essence of who we are. It is a very crucial entity and very few persons are able to comprehend this energy fully or express what it is all about in the right words. Its definition is so vast that it encompasses the universe, God, and the individual, all as one whole and complete in the form of non-dual, absolute intelligence energy. The way science is related to the cognitive mind, spirituality is related to the intuitive mind. The spirit is simply the presence of this awareness, flowing through consciousness, residing in the mind and body. Everything depends on any individual's intensity of this aware energy, which differs from one human being to another.

Therefore I repeat that awareness is the state of our being; it manifests itself in the mind, making it aware so that it can become conscious and retain its role, independently, as the witnessing self. The role of the cognitive mind is to first become aware and consciously separate this energy into two in order to choose and experience what it perceives. Psychic experiences via the intellect relate that to its opposites and take over in self-interest for the mind to realize its own internal consciousness.

To summarize: awareness is non-dual intelligence energy; it shows *who* we are. The moment it attaches itself to the mind, it dissipates into thoughts of duality forming our consciousness, experiencing and realizing, becoming *what* we are.

***

Awareness is purely existential, manifesting itself only in 'the now', spontaneously observing the universe as it is. It emerges in the field of wholeness to play the game of dual existence, separating into its polarity within space, time and matter. It is the absolute non-dual energy, experiencing through the mind its separation in duality and further becoming aware of its own individual awareness, which has now become conscious to realize what life is all about. It is only when consciousness reaches its original stage of oneness in total purity, as the absolute non-dual, that it is equated with awareness, the energy in its absoluteness.

***

Many who are knowledgeable on the subject of spirituality are convinced that they are spiritually realized; intellectually, they could be, but, in actuality, it is only that experience in self-surrender, which relieves us from all the attachments that we are bound to. The knowledgeable ones do not apprehend that this subject demands absoluteness through acts of pure selflessness, compassion and oneness, devoid of any identification and attachments. Only then would our intensity of awareness expand in totality and our consciousness experience a transformation from the ego to the divine. Spiritual realization signifies the end of individual identification. The destination arrives only when we are aware and conscious in totality, reaching the status of God realization, which is extremely rare.

***

We should always remember that the mind can be our best friend or our worst foe. In the former case, awareness is its saviour and, in the latter case, the ego, which stirs up desires and greed for material possessions, leads us towards suffering and misery.

There are very few who will relate to awareness as the ultimate in providing the essence, meaning and subject of life. We should never forget that every human mind needs awareness to be conscious about how to expand and evolve from its separateness from nature and attain oneness to realize *what* we are.

***

Today, we will find a huge variety of teachings and preaching offering us all kinds of solutions for our seemingly endless problems. But we will seldom come across someone who is trying to convey the message that we come from the dark energy of our universe representing nothing and go back into the same. The state of our being is in awareness, whereas the quality of our being is in consciousness. Both combine as one to transform our existence and lead us towards divinity, so long as we are aware of the same.

There is no need for us to seek liberation, enlightenment, moksha or those fancy states of God realization. There is nothing there to seek; all that is there lies within for us to experience in awareness and realize with consciousness.

All that we need is intense awareness to self-experience and realize, and create that divine uniqueness, laying the basis for our individuality to remain in eternity. The presence of our awareness residing within will rise and shine, subtly guiding us to reveal the secret of absolute truth, love and oneness, which we perceive as God.

Chapter 15

ARE WE INTELLECTUALS?

The intuitive mind is a sacred gift and the rational mind is a faithful servant. We have created a society that honors the servant and has forgotten the gift ...

— Albert Einstein

It took me a long time to understand the difference between *intelligence* and *intellect*. They are so close yet so far apart. Both terms describe mental ability, allowing the mind to explore the complexities of existence, yet they have their distinct differences. When I noticed how intellectuals missed the simplest of things or how they were prejudiced against accepting anything new, given their preconditioned beliefs, I pondered over the subject to understand the differences in the framework of our minds with regard to the basic link between logic and meditation on the one hand and intuitiveness with imitation on the other. Let me elucidate further.

Intellect is the faculty of questioning, reasoning, analysing, choosing and deciding through knowledge, thoughts, ideas and emotions. It is the capacity of knowing as well as the ability to decipher cognition and arrive at psychic conclusions. It collects data from the memory bank of past knowledge, studies it and separates a subject into its relative duality. This gives the mind the freedom to choose between one and the other polar opposite for its self-interest with regard to desires and emotions. It is of great significance in our material existence.

Intelligence is an inborn quality and comes prior to intellect. It reveals the degree of spontaneous awareness in a person. It is unique to each individual and is the guru within, pointing the intellect in the direction through sheer commonsense to undertake its activities such as reasoning and analysing. It enlightens our creativity, imagination and intuitiveness and turns them into a reality. It shows us the way to solve logical and emotional problems of the intellect.

Intelligence is wholesome; intellect separates that completeness for the sake of physical and material benefits in self-identification. Intellect transmits borrowed information, gathering data from various sources, storing that in our memory from which it constantly extracts information.

***

In our day-to-day life, we often notice that individuals, especially those possessing higher knowledge, while interacting with others, will definitely try and impress those with lesser knowledge. This is natural because the net content of the mind is nothing but ego.

Those with higher knowledge are considered to be intellectuals possessing greater intellect. They are highly acclaimed in the material world and win numerous accolades of honour. But in the spiritual realm, an intellectual is treated as merely carrying exhausted knowledge and beliefs, prejudiced in his own way of thinking. There is no openness, freshness, newness or aliveness in intellectuals. For instance, in India, we come across an assortment of 'intellectuals' who keep on repeating our ancient scriptures, again and again, with nothing new to add.

***

The higher the awareness, the greater shall be our intelligence. How similar it is to life, which flows in a flux with an aura of uncertainty, which can only be experienced but not defined. If we happen to ask any scientist or a technologist about the source/s of their discoveries, we might be surprised by their response. Without giving any credit to their mind or its intellect, they will lay more stress on those hunches with flashes of intuition, admitting that something beyond their mind was responsible for their discoveries.

We should remember that if a person keeps depending upon his personal intellect and blind beliefs with a conditioned and rigid mind, he is bound to follow and imitate others. But if he is spontaneous, he will stake his intuitiveness in order to learn about and experience life on his own. The awareness of an intelligent person increases with exposure, experience and basic commonsense.

Those who are uninformed may not be knowledgeable, but their basic intelligence gained through experiences in meditative awareness will amaze us. There will be instances when we can get the best advice and guidance from our helpers at home, though they may be hardly literate. However, they could be wise and experienced enough to help in solving many of our problems. On the other hand, an intellectual relies more upon his limited data of knowledge gained on subjects, which interest him, and may not have dealt with the harsh realities of life.

***

In today's world, there is no shortage of intellectuals constantly offering recycled knowledge on various subjects. What is scarce is basic commonsense, which is becoming so uncommon. Commonsense requires basic intelligence, which is independent of any specialized or specified knowledge. If commonsense were to be given its proper value and respect, there would be far less wrongdoing; but it is just the opposite that is happening.

When the intellect takes over, reasoning and judgement get impaired possibly due to borrowed knowledge based upon others' experiences, making one's own commonsense go haywire. Commonsense has become so elusive and seemingly redundant that even most of those in the government and various other institutions/organizations under its aegis, in many instances, lack this quality. Probably as they have their own vested interests, they are more inclined towards following their intellect rather than using their commonsense and intelligence.

***

Besides commonsense, there are qualities such as imagination and intuitiveness accompanying intelligence, providing newer ideas for us to evolve and ascend to higher realms. They finally culminate along with intellect to form our intent in order to experience life to the fullest, revealing the level of our integrity in any act. What matters the most here is whether this psychic process is going through a proactive or reactive approach. In the former, intelligence takes over and, in the latter, the intellect reacts under the influence of emotional desires, based on selfish interests.

Intuition and imagination, though differing in their characteristics, come prior to cognitive thoughts. The former is the voice of the spirit being the Self, whereas the latter is a fantasy of the intellect.

Imagination is when we visualize a wide range of images and concepts in response to what we desire. *Intuition*, on the other hand, is immediate along with spontaneous awareness, striking our mind with a flash of fresh energy, before the occurrence of any other psychic process.

In other words, intuition is that instinctual experience providing the ability to know things without using our intellect. It always happens in the present moment. In comparison, *intellect* is that power of reasoning, borrowing intelligence from here and there, and from past accumulated data, in order to choose and formulate what we desire. Lastly, *intention* is that determination to fulfil a certain objective in a particular way.

Imagination is fantasizing how far our creative mind can soar, and, if backed by intellect, can transform our dreams into reality. Intuition is far greater, penetrating the mind by utilizing fresh cosmic intelligence, prior to anything else.

Intuition is like our third eye, sixth sense or fourth dimension, whatever we may wish to call it. For example, many times, just by seeing a person, we seem to know instantaneously a lot about him or her, without having to analyse our thoughts and emotions through our intellect.

***

We also have *integrity*, which, if applied either through intelligence or the intellect, reflects the overall wholeness or purity of any act of ours. In establishing ourselves, integrity becomes our code of conduct, revealing our totality of character and our overall personality through our behaviour, mannerisms and actions.

All said and done, we have vibrant intelligence called awareness percolating through intuition, imagination, intellect, intention and integrity, revealing the various processes of the miraculous machine called the mind. Each has its own distinct role to play; some perform by creating new thoughts whilst others by utilizing borrowed information from the memory bank or from any other source. How to tap and cultivate them in their right perspective is the art of living.

***

It is imperative that we know our mind through logic as well as meditation: how to experience the outer world through science and the inner world through spirituality. In order to balance the two sensitively, we should opt for both but we must remember that intelligence will take over from the intellect when it comes to uniting our consciousness with integrity.

Chapter 16

The Flow of Life

Life is a series of natural and spontaneous changes. Don't resist them – that only creates sorrow. Let reality be reality. Let things flow naturally forward in whatever way they like.

— Lao Tzu*

Life is full of surprises; it can be sedate one moment and tumultuous the next! Hence, it is best to go with the flow of life. No matter how much we plan either for today or tomorrow, anything can happen at any time to disturb the rhythm of our planning. We may be in the best of moods when we get up in the morning after enjoying a nice, deep sleep. Everything can go haywire if any unfavourable event takes place suddenly. Such an event can shatter our day, spoil our mood and ruin all our seemingly well-laid plans. Whether we like it or not, in this world, the only thing that is certain is death and that which remains uncertain is what we call life.

The more we resist the flow of life, the longer the agony to be endured. Even as I am writing this chapter, I

---

*Lao Tzu (606–531 B.C.), a renowned Chinese philosopher and writer, was the founder of Taoism (a Chinese philosophy advocating humility and piety).

am looking out of a window facing a river. I am watching a swimmer applying all his strength to go upstream against a strong current. He is reaching nowhere; he is, in fact, stationary in spite of all efforts. He seems to be struggling to prove that he can defy the pressure of the tide just to satisfy his ego. Such an attitude may not be always beneficial.

Life provides a certain flow to each one of us throughout our existence, from birth to death, expecting us to go along with it. We may call this destiny or circumstance but we need to fulfil our journey of life to the best of our ability in order to facilitate the source of aliveness within us. Of course, sometimes it is challenging to go against the flow, just to test our resilience.

***

All of us try our best to implement and succeed in our plans. However, life has a strange way of deviating from our thought processes in its own direction. We may get angry, dejected or stressed, but it seems advisable to surrender our ego and accept the realities of life, as they are, moment to moment. Life has its own way of confronting us with bouts of circumstantial experiences, whether favourable or not. We are supposed to accept what life gives us, instead of trying to mould it in the way we would want to.

We should make efforts, by all means, to change negative experiences; we should not let them dishearten us if the results are not as per our expectations.

***

All that we are required to do is to be alert, attentive and aware in order to remain centred in whatever we think and do. I was once a businessman controlling a sizable, profitable enterprise for many years. Life took a sudden turn and I gave it up, and for what? Something clicked in my mind, the direction of the flow changed; I picked up my pen and started writing on the subject that I was always passionate about (spirituality). Those who knew me could never imagine I could ever switch over to such a field, which, for average personalities, does not offer ample profits. But here I am, busy writing a series of books with the same zeal as I started a few years back on the first one.

Therefore, we should not be afraid to make any dramatic changes if life demands or our heart desires; we should go with that flow, especially when our gut feeling and passions agree with that change. At times, besides running after money in order to fulfil our desires for material possessions and luxuries, we also need to listen to our heart and soul. We may have made great plans in our current situation, which I agree are essential. However, there is no hard and fast rule that we cannot retract and start afresh looking for any other new opportunity that life may offer us. After all, what is life? It is simply a motion of energy, which is characterized by changes.

We should always remember that we just cannot control all that we wish to; we should not get disheartened by the occasional failure, but should be consistently aware. Our intellect will intervene and our ego will pressurize us to resist any change and fight against our status quo, but even if we manage to counter them, we will not be able to go against the flow of life for long. It is best to surrender our ego and accept our situation as it stands at present. After all, existence is predominant at any given moment as it is; we need to adhere to the realm we are in and try to be more existential rather than keep brooding over the past or the future. With total conviction in a state of alert awareness and being conscious of every moment, we must make the best out of what life demands from us. We should go in for self-contemplation regularly by being alert and attentive; this action will keep us focused and aware.

***

When we become angry, frustrated or upset, we should just take a deep breath to calm ourselves. We will then enter the presence of 'the now' and will be in a better position to tackle any unfavourable situation. Spirituality basically teaches us that it is best to stop clinging to what we are attached and withdraw in order not to obstruct the flow of life. Non-attachment is the ultimate antidote to all our sufferings.

We normally get trapped in a vicious cycle involving attachments to our emotional links and material accumulations and are unable to break free. We cling on to them desiring more and more, thereby restricting the flow of life. Spirituality says let go; with the exhalation of each breath, we should have faith in the next one that we inhale. We should voluntarily give up our attachments and, with complete conviction, face what life has in store for us. We should go into the arena of life with our eyes wide open, but with love and gratitude.

***

Conscious breathing itself ensures the smooth flow of life, which, if practised properly, can still our thoughts and generate that vitality in the present moment so essential to all of us. We should simply dwell in such moments with more mindfulness and with less concern about the past or future. Our true home is in 'the now', with every breath awakening us to experience all that is there in this very moment: from our family to each of our belongings. As mentioned earlier, life may not always give us what we want, but we should not go against its flow and resist, for our persistence will only make it more difficult and strenuous for us.

We should go with the waves; at times, crashing against the boulders on the shore, become one with them, roll back again and face new challenges that life throws up in order to gain experience and evolve with every passing moment. We are a part of the ocean of cosmic intelligence; every situation will develop as ordained by a higher power, whether we like it or not. We should keep this reality in mind that life is not a bed of roses. But how we live and evolve as a result of our experiences in the bed of thorns is what life is all about.

When we discover the significance of living existentially, from one moment to the next, only then will the flow of life become natural and smooth. Our thoughts on the past and the present are bound to create a disturbance with all the chattering (of thoughts) within the mind. We should learn the art of acceptance with the surrender of the ego; otherwise our resistance will only go against the flow.

***

We all know it is not right to lie or cheat; yet many of us do so to amass wealth and the luxuries it can buy. While fulfilling only our self-interest, we have become indifferent and insensitive to the serene flow of life. Our mind builds up an illusory reality; we get captivated by material possessions and target everything we come across only for what we will get in exchange for what we give. The world is made up of givers and takers. We should try to become a giver, for it is in giving that we receive.

Apart from the mind, even society at large will force us to go against the flow so as to acquire that illusory life suffused with sybaritic pleasures. In pursuit of such a life, we end up frustrated and miserable, as the pleasures are only temporary. That is why we are ultimately left with only one choice: to follow the spiritual path that provides lasting peace and tranquillity. As mentioned earlier, we should go inwards, surrender our 'me-and-mine' ego and, with awareness, walk this path, sincerely and purposefully.

***

Life always has a deeper meaning for us. We should look around us, observe, be aware and intuit; we should stop thinking about yesterday and tomorrow. A serene reflection of 'who and what we are' will follow, and that is what the flow of life is all about. It is not about being perfect, successful or always making the right choices at the right time. It is about being aware and conscious of all that we do in every moment, learning from those experiences at every step that we take during this flow.

***

In the play of life created by the mind under the influence of maya (illusion), we should celebrate our life to the fullest, but with our third eye open in order to experience every moment. We should go with the tide and not against it. We should not utilize every situation only in our self-interest or this flow will go astray. If we tread the spiritual path, a natural course will emerge, where instead of our analytical mind, a surge of spontaneous awareness shall guide us all the way. We should give as much as possible and find joy in that act for, according to St Francis of Assisi*: 'It is in giving that you receive … it is in dying that you are born to an eternal life.'

---

*Saint Francis of Assisi (1181/1182 to 1226) was a respected Italian Roman Catholic preacher.

Chapter 17

THE FLOW OF ENERGY

Energy can't be created or destroyed, and energy flows. It must be in a direction, with some kind of internal, emotive, spiritual direction. It must have some effect somewhere.

— Keanu Reeves*

What is energy? It is the basic but ultimate ingredient, which powers this universe. It remains absolute and changeless in its fundamental character; however, within itself, it changes into many different forms having their own characteristics – thermal, electrical, chemical, nuclear and so on. As we are taught in school-level physics, when static or stored, energy is referred to as potential and, in motion, kinetic. Energy is the ability to move a certain force into its field to do any work. In its kinetic state, it is interchangeable from one form to another and can be derived from various sources. The Sun, for example, is the source of energy for life on Earth. It releases mainly enormous quantities of light energy as well as thermal and heat energy.

***

*Keanu Reeves (born 2 September 1964) is a Canadian actor, director, musician and philanthropist.

Every motion or act requires energy to sustain and propagate itself. Energy is the fundamental entity in this universe, which remains constant and cannot be created or destroyed. It is transmitted, stored, applied and transformed from one form to another. Matter or a mass of body is a form of energy vibrating in different frequencies, which, when arrested, manifests itself or changes from one form to another.

Life is one such form of aware energy, which is transmitted from the core of its being called awareness to its subtle field referred to as consciousness. Both manifest themselves in the mind and reside in a gross form of energy as the body.

Awareness is the essence of our being and consciousness is the crux of our acquiring a unique individuality. They both combine and reflect our transformation during life from child consciousness to later experience ego, with the aim and vision to eventually realize divine consciousness.

***

Consciousness flows through the physical, intellectual and emotional fields, attaching itself to all the relativities of existence within a defined human spiritual sphere. Even though over 90 per cent of our acts are done unconsciously, the remaining 10 per cent are done consciously, setting human beings apart from all other living creatures. Not only that, our consciousness, besides being the basis of our experiences and linking all information to our senses, also has the capability to bond itself to a universal field of consciousness. This stream of aware conscious energy flows in the path of least resistance and requires a constant balancing from our physical, mental and spiritual faculties. If this flow of energy gets imbalanced, stagnant or blocked, we experience what is referred to as suffering or disease.

Therefore, if we are conscious of our flow of energy, whether it is flowing free or blocked, we can modulate and harmonize our body and mind. Normally, in most cases, what we notice is that in the midst of material existence, consciousness or the spirit is not in consonance with the mind and the body. When our consciousness is low and is in conflict with our mind, it has negative effects on our overall distribution of different forms of energies flowing from their own respective centres. In other words, the energy transmitted at such times is affected by our conflict-prone state of consciousness.

***

The way in which nutritious food and proper exercises provide extra energy to improve our physical health, similarly, a positive attitude enhances the psychic flow. We also need to be aware of those inert spiritual energies like kundalini* and chakras,** the vital energy centres, whether they are in tune with our body and mind or not.

***

After all, what is life? It is simply a kinetic flow of aware energy, coming from nothing, passing through our body and brain and going back into that nothing. It is aware conscious energy, which gives us something called existence that makes us alive and the flow of these conscious moments becomes everything for us. This

---

*Kundalini (meaning 'the coiled one') refers to a form of primal energy (or shakti) believed to be located at the base of the spine.
**Chakras (meaning wheels) refer to those parts of the body said to be psychic-energy centres.

everything is something because it represents and also connects to that infinite formless energy, taking care of us even as the mind expands and evolves – physically, mentally and spiritually.

***

Raw energy, after it manifests itself in our mind, flows in two different directions. The first is towards desires for material attachments and possessions, taking us closer to an illusory lifestyle called the false self. This is referred to as the ego projecting itself as 'I, me, mine and myself'. Such a flow creates our outward personality in the materialistic world.

The second direction of flow expands our spiritual self, character and personal power, resulting in the formation our inner unique individuality. This makes us realize who and what we really are, away from the illusory mind, and is called the 'witnessing self'. The spiritual flow of energy is fundamentally our actual reality, representing the presence of our inner being in awareness. It journeys from the lower to the higher self, from the material to the spiritual, from passion to compassion and from the sexual attractions to the awareness in higher consciousness.

In the material stage, the flow gets limited by our thoughts, identifies itself with the human body and its presence revolves around duality, functioning mainly in our self-interest. This concept of the mind is referred to as the flow of ego. It constantly changes within a specified space and time, from positive to negative or vice versa, attaching itself either to the past or the future and forgetting the present; it is an emotional flow and oscillates between pleasure and pain.

In the spiritual stage, we have awareness signifying the presence of our real being. Here the perceptual experiences of our consciousness take us inwards, towards the subject of life. This flow of energy evolves from the personal to the impersonal and from separateness towards oneness; this is an experiential journey leading us towards divine consciousness into a unified field of undivided wholeness. This presence of awareness gradually transcends into a higher consciousness, reaching its final stage after realizing its totality in purity, which, spiritually, we refer to as the Self or God realization.

***

To understand the difference between the flow of the spirit and the ego, we can find innumerable books on this subject written by philosophers and spiritual gurus. In my opinion, even if we prefer one to the other, it still remains a very personal experiential journey to attain this flow and, individually to know, experience and realize what life is all about.

Unless we transcend from the lower plane to the higher one, it becomes difficult to comprehend the difference. Both flows manifest themselves in the mind and the manner we utilize or balance these two depends entirely upon the intensity of any individual awareness. Both are required in life and, as we mature with age, the right experience and wisdom from each prove beneficial.

The first type is for acquiring constructive materialism in separateness to provide daily comforts and the latter is for peace and joy through the feeling of oneness for all.

***

The ego becomes an essential part of our materialistic existence making our raw energy vibrant and alive. As long as we use the ego for constructive purposes, it is highly beneficial.

The ego is that power, which provides the impetus, the drive and the ambition to achieve something beyond the mundane and the ordinary. It is vital to material progress, especially in establishing us in the midst of competition.

However, when the ego makes us swollen headed and tries to convince us that we are superior to others, it overpowers our mind and starts to control it. It then becomes negative and destructive. An unconscious ego is that power of mind, which is functioning purely in self-interest, trying to prove its superiority over others. To keep such a selfish ego in check, we need to be constantly observant of the flow of energy. We, being that source of our individual awareness, need to be alert and aware of our own mind. When ego becomes negative, we are supposed to counter-balance it with a positive flow of spiritual energy to avoid suffering, pain and disease.

***

Happiness and sadness are a part of life, the first boosting our energy and the second depleting it. They both are relative and originate from the vagaries of the mind. Our job is to keep the objective independent from the two aforementioned separate flows and be constantly aware of them. We need to surrender our mind, accept the reality and bring these two flows together from where they separated. We need to be aware and conscious of both so that we neither go overboard with excitement or ecstasy nor get overly troubled when one of the flows becomes excessive.

***

In order to be spiritual, the flow of aware energy requires spontaneity for it to flow proactively. The flow of psychic energy is depleted when the mind, instead of being in the present moment, starts to brood over the past and think about the future. Proactive people are imaginative, intuitive and creative. They do not let go of the present moment by wasting their time in reacting to any situation.

In reactive people, the mind responds with self-interest; emotionally and calculatingly, indulging in thinking more about what it is going to gain or lose in the future rather than focusing its flow of energy on the present.

***

Success is highly seductive; almost everyone who achieves it tends to forget the qualities that led to it. The flow of energy in any egoist starts to diminish with this new-found trophy, unless the mind is aware to keep the flow of energy in check. Virtually all of us want more and more money and material possessions. Being dissatisfied and frustrated with our present circumstances, at times, we tend to adopt all kinds of dubious means, including snatching others' wealth or property, in order to fulfil our ambitions. Such a step leads to a sense of false self. This is the stage at which the failure of success starts; the egoistic mind thinks it is supreme. On the other hand, it is also only after we realize the shortcomings of being an egoist that we transcend into a state of spirituality, where the energy flow is filled with compassion, wholeness and awareness of our truth and reality.

***

Let us now, in contrast to the negative energy, consider the spiritual flow of energy, which is far more alive, creative and unlimited than what our sensory thoughts can perceive. It is relayed from the prefrontal neo-cortex part of the brain, the part that links the physical intellect with the spirit or intuition and also to the power of the subconscious, our very special personal power. This flow emanates from deep within us. This is the power of our intention, our purpose, our ultimate aim, our character and our integrity, exhibiting a combination of psychic and spiritual energies.

I repeat: there are two distinct levels in the mind. In the first level, all data fed through our sensory organs is energized in a domain called 'I', which thinks and then acts. It leads us to perform various actions and points us towards desires and attachments in self-interest. The second level entails the flow of positive energy, which is intense, intuitive and potent. It is the divine energy of awareness behaving as the witnessing self, guiding us, especially when we are about to do something wrong. It elevates us to a higher level of consciousness, strongly, subtly and silently, thereby helping us in witnessing our own mind.

Such an infinite flow of awareness settles within our subconscious as the divine power, differing in its degree over time and consolidating our own individual personal power. That is why I simply call it personal power rather than use any other confusing synonym. I do not know much about the eternity of soul. However, I definitely know that the body and the mind will wither one day and it is my personal power, which shall create an individuality that remains forever in accordance to its deeds. From the compassionate Buddha to the tyrannical Adolf Hitler, their bodies have perished, but the legacies of their individualities, through their personal power (whether positive or negative), remain alive even today and shall do so till eternity.

We should always remember that the creation of this personal power deep within us should be our purpose and ultimate aim. It is our divinity within, revealing the intention, character and flow of our energy. It is for us to decide when to take this flow of energy into higher levels or lower levels of consciousness to discover the divine or the devil residing within. We should never let this flow take us to that unconscious stage where we do not feel worthy of ourselves.

***

Quantum physicists claim that our world is all energy, constantly flowing and unchanging in its fundamental ingredient. They also claim that this energy comes from nothing, turning into form, matter or physical existence, and then goes back into nothing. The theological view is that God, who is eternal, created this universe. God is absolute and omnipresent, flowing from one form into another. Spirituality describes this flow of energy as the source of creation, where God and creation are not two but one in a flow of aware and conscious kinetic energy called life.

Energy, however, is an infinite flow coming in and going out of physical matter. It moves like the way water flows, crossing huge rocks and boulders and disperses with uncertainty in its random flow. Life is such a movement of energy; it moves arbitrarily, unless it is kept in check by awareness. How we see and what we think of our universe is possible only after we become aware and conscious of such a flow. Awareness is such a state of mind; otherwise whatever exists all around would be utterly meaningless.

***

As mentioned earlier, life is nothing but a flow of energy. The origin and maintenance of life have been attributed to the flow of light and heat energy provided by the Sun. We notice a certain rhythm and circularity in any flow of energy. It keeps on expanding and evolving spirally, revealing itself within the vortex of its movement. In that spiral motion, we have a circumference where there is no beginning or end; the movement can be never-ending. This is how life keeps flowing, expanding and advancing with every birth and rebirth. Each death brings forth a new beginning, clarifying that there is no end to life. Each seed is allocated its respective evolvement in every physical existence, producing many more seeds to expand further, according to their own capacities.

***

The universe, as we know, is a sea of energy, vibrating at different frequencies and flowing in spiritual, psychic and physical forms. We have the ability to absorb, transfer and utilize this energy creating our own field through the energy centres provided to us. The degrees of balance of these centres depend upon the synergy among the body, mind and spirit. Energy, as claimed by spirituality, moves throughout our body from seven energy-spinning centres in a vortex called chakras (wheels). These chakras are aroused through tantras (methods of attaining a higher awareness of consciousness) correlating that with specific mantras (sacred sounds) focusing on certain geometric patterns called yantras.

***

Prana, the vital energy force, enters the body through the breath in the top from the sahasrara (crown chakra) and travels down into muladhara (root chakra). In most cases, it remains passive, unless it starts to move upwards, referred to as kundalini (defined earlier in this chapter). When energy travels upward through our respective chakras in a serpent-like manner, it encounters physiological and psychological obstructions. The aforementioned seven chakras are aligned vertically along our back from the top of our head till the bottom of our spine.

In order to optimize the flow of energies, these chakras have to be opened, balanced and tuned through meditative awareness, pranayama (the practice of controlling the breath) and yoga. This entire process is referred to as kundalini yoga, which is tantric in nature. The purpose is to integrate our lower consciousness with the upper consciousness. In this manner, the energy from the lower chakra rises from the base of our spine towards the sahasrara chakra at the top. This experience, if realized, provides us with the boundless energy of love in the higher consciousness.

***

Energy – solar, hydro, thermal, electrical, chemical, nuclear and so on – flows through everything, but the ultimate and the most intense force of aware energy flow through us. Everyone experiences it differently and that is how we differ from each other. When energy is free and subtle, the flow is spirited and increases our vitality. We experience a variety of flows – meditative, creative, psychic and emotional – from dense to luminous in our human system. How we facilitate or impede this flow is the art of life. It is up to us to create the life we want. We should allow the energy to flow freely, get rid of negative emotions and agitations and let go of our personalized ego (which creates desires for unnecessary material attachments). We should always be alert and attentive to observe, experience and realize with awareness how the universal energy is flowing through us.

Chapter 18

Here and Now

I am sitting in front of a breathtaking scenery: mountains in the front, and a river flowing below. The Sun is about to set. Hues of orange dot the sky. Heaven is right here on earth. Then why does my mind continue to wander in thoughtless thoughts? Try as I may, I can't keep it still. Why?

— Gian Kumar

Many spiritual teachers, in fact, all of them, emphasize on the principle of living in 'the now'. What I am presenting here is nothing new; the intention is more to stress upon the significance of this principle in our everyday life.

***

Our mind refuses to be still for more than a few moments, darting back and forth between the past and future; so we need to be mindful in order to be able to absorb better whatever that is happening around us right now.

Our attention is normally distracted and we begin multitasking so many times that what we anticipate invariably does not materialize. We live for the future, depending upon on our past and forgetting the present. The mind is a daydreaming machine; incessant thoughts are constantly ruminating on past knowledge and projecting that into the future, presuming itself to be in 'the now'. The mind, through its thoughts, can never capture the present. The moment the mind receives, processes and transmits thoughts on what it perceives, a new 'now' will take its place.

***

The present is always existential; everything is happening as it should, but the mind is unable to perceive the same. Likewise, existence prevails in the present, and that is the fundamental reality. During daytime, it is in the present that the Sun shines, birds sing, rivers flow and nature reveals its treasures, but, by the time our mind registers any of these happenings, the present becomes the past. Time is a method to measure and record the changes in our environment. It is the duration of movement represented by clocks, watches and other devices and the period of 'twenty-four hours' is based on one rotation of the Earth on its axis around the Sun.

Time is flowing constantly and continuously; it is real in 'the now'. However, this 'now' is constantly being updated; the past has been established, we have the immediate 'now' and the future is waiting to become the present. There is an awareness of something, possibly the power of our observation and the state of our mind, which permits us to measure the relationship among time, space, and the speed at which time moves and the distance we cover in a specified time. However, this activity is restricted only to our physical reality and is of a temporary nature.

***

The quality of awareness in each person is represented by the level of consciousness, which we all know is not physical; hence it has no effect on the duration of time. It deciphers everything through experiencing every moment as it is. In the universe, we have only absoluteness. There is only one moment in which the presence of everything or nothing exists. All that happens in this universe is in this very moment and time is a measure of the indefinite continued progression of its physical existence that occurs in an irreversible succession from the past to the present to the future. Therefore, our journey of life represents a state of time eventually to enter into a state of timelessness.

***

Physics is a subject that deals with the physicality of things, where consciousness does not fit in. Awareness and consciousness are inner subjective experiences, of which science today has little knowledge. These two can exist as everything and nothing simultaneously, having no direct connection to space, time and its speed. Life and death, time and timelessness, sound and silence: all are inclusive in the wholeness of that absolute of nothingness. Unless we are inwardly alert, we can easily get lost in this play of polarities. It is primarily for this reason we are supposed to stay alert in order to become aware and then be attentive about that alertness to become conscious. After all spirituality is nothing but the art of being conscious from one moment to the next.

This duration of awareness cannot be measured by chronological time, which the mind undertakes to become conscious and experience any situation. In reality, there is no past or future but only the presence of our attention, moment to moment. Therefore, at one end, what we have is a realm of the mind, which is designated by time and in the other sphere, which is beyond the cognitive mind, a state of timelessness. It is in meditative awareness that we go beyond perception, observe and experience timelessness. Since the mind cannot be in 'the now', let us see how the presence of awareness in any individual gets affected every moment revealing his state of consciousness.

In spiritual terms, except for the present moment, everything else is an illusion. Since spirituality does not consider the phenomenon of time, what exists is only a continuous present. The mind, through its thoughts, deceives us by connecting the present to the past and projecting it into the future, claiming itself to be in the present. To be in the present moment, one needs to exist without thinking, for thoughts are always of the past.

We should observe each moment, focused with complete attention, so that the mind is in total awareness of that experience without thinking, as it is. We will then know that in the presence of any moment, time has no meaning.

From the spiritual point of view, there is only one eternal or present time, in which our presence exists and we experience life. We have to utilize this conceptual construction of experience more in psychological time, living not by the measurement of chronology, but from one moment to the next, under the strict observance of our presence. We will then begin to watch things more clearly, not get drawn into what the mind is thinking and projecting from the past into the future, but by being alert and aware, witnessing what is happening in the present moment.

***

Spiritualism provides us methods to break the barriers of time to enter the internal perception of witnessing our mind in a neutral manner. We simply transcend beyond the thoughts of the past and future, living from one moment to the next. This process teaches us how to slow down the external perception of the mind, thereby meditatively living in awareness through observance with watchfulness, without following any chronological order.

The experience of meditation surpasses all other factors because we are alive existentially and we see everything in totality rather than perceiving parts of reality in restricted space and time.

***

Our thoughts take shape as a result of our accumulated knowledge based on entities such as beliefs, faith, ideas, imagination and concepts given or passed on by others for us to follow. These entities go back to centuries of old traditions, conditioned by various factors of the past, forming rigid opinions and judgements about different topics, thereby forming our personality.

If we learn and follow the methods given by spiritualism, and not relate the present with the past or the future, we will truly be able to harness its spontaneous potentiality and convert that into its actuality. Spontaneous awareness obtained existentially in each moment is the culmination of truth in creativity. It is obtained through thoughtless thoughts without the intellect interfering to make us choose either this or that option in any situation.

***

Mindfulness is an ongoing process of the mind in the present, which allows us to go beneath its periphery. It is that required duration without any measurement, experiencing in totality every situation from one moment to the next. This is one of the best ways to keep the mind away from suffering due to thoughts from the past and uncertainties of the future. An ignorant, unconscious mind is filled with desires and emotions, constantly obsessed and attached to self-interest.

In order to observe the truth, we need to witness our own mind and shake off the clouds of emotions that surround us. We will notice that the mind is generally lost in the external world, battered by chattering thoughts, depending on past beliefs and speculating on the future that it desires. In order to stop this cycle of distraction, we need to oppose this habit right from the beginning, bringing mind into the focus of 'the now'.

Once we are able to comprehend what needs to be done by not thinking emotionally about the past and the future, our presence will be nearer to the truth of any particular situation. Say, somebody has upset us; instead of getting into a chain of agitated emotional thoughts against that person, we should cut off our thoughts and, instead, carefully study our disturbed mind. We will immediately grasp how miserable the mind was making us feel in reaction to that incident and getting imprisoned by that situation. In fact, we will become aware of our reaction and proactively decide on what needs to be done pragmatically.

***

Mindfulness, i.e., being in the present moment, enables us to see clearly what is happening around us every moment. It helps us to direct our thoughts properly, sustain them and act spontaneously without any evaluation with complete confidence in our creative awareness. The training begins by watching attentively any situation and observing how our mind reacts to what it is experiencing. Our mind should converge like a spotlight on an object, with attention focused on one particular experience, rather than hopping and skipping here and there.

Controlling the breath is another method. Once we become aware of our breathing rhythm, it relaxes us and silences the chattering of thoughts. It awakens us and enables us to handle any distracting situation in a tranquil manner.

***

As mentioned earlier, life exists always in 'the now'; if we wish to experience joy, it has to be in this moment. A true spiritual awakening is realized not by reading books, listening to a guru or knowing and repeating Sanskrit shlokas with blind beliefs. Admittedly, these factors cannot be dismissed, but awakening is an experiential phenomenon, which is realized only in 'the here and now'. It is a state of consciousness, which, if not awakened, we will be ruled by the thinking, but wavering, mind.

Thinking is uncontrollable and we can never be in a no-mind zone, unless of course, when we are in deep sleep. The mind is designed for thinking; we get weighed down with thoughts and, under that burden, we do not see anything as it really is. What we normally see are distorted images; being biased and prejudiced, we keep on thinking incessantly about concepts and images in blind belief, judging this and that, for fulfilling selfish desires.

Therefore, the mind needs to be trained to balance the past, present and the future in totality as one for our overall well-being. Do not reject any of the three, but also do not keep brooding on the past or future. The present needs to be experienced in such a manner, where the observer combines all three into one. Thoughts, which will arise during such moments, will be choiceless, meaning, without any discrimination.

Spiritual awakening is a systematic and progressive process, where the quality of thinking is heightened by 'the here and now', being more in tune with the present. The mind, rather than being in 'the now', keeps adding excessive burdens by incessantly thinking about the past and the future.

Eventually, when awakened, we become a witness to our own thoughts and regulate them accordingly. The awakening keeps happening in 'the now' and our state of consciousness, instead of identifying itself with the body and the mind, transcends into the presence of our awareness, allowing that moment to be as it is. There is no greater spiritual experience than being in 'the here and now'; we strongly need to practise, balance and control our thoughts to realize that attainment of a serene state.

Chapter 19

LIFE ... A PARADOX

Day after day countless people die. Yet the living wish to live forever. O Lord, what can be a greater wonder?

— Yudhishtir*

A paradox is a statement or concept that is seemingly contradictory, yet seems to be true. It can also be described as a statement that is self-contradictory, which, at first, seems to be true. In the spiritual context, it becomes imperative to understand the true meaning behind paradoxes in order for us to realize the illusions, which the mind creates. According to Hinduism, the mind is that supernatural power by which the universe becomes manifest. Maya is that illusion or appearance of the magnificent world created by the phenomenal mind.

***

*In the epic Mahabharata (written by the erudite Ved Vyas), Yudhishtir (or Yudhishthira) was the eldest son of Pandu (the king of Hastinapura in ancient India) and Kunti (the queen). Yudhishtir had four brothers. Together, they were called the Pandavas. Yudhishtir was known for his unflinching honesty.

We live in a world of paradoxes, where things are seldom what they seem to be. This axiom is valid for most aspects of our lives, since our existence is dependent upon dualities or opposites. In order to define or understand anything, we have to rely on its dichotomy and relate that to something meaningful for us. So what is real or good for one person may be unreal and bad for another.

The meaning of life would not exist without knowing about death. This is where paradoxes come in, confusing us and making our lives imbalanced.

***

Polarity is necessary in everyday life. The mind needs to relate one extreme to another, the manner in which it is required for a question to have an answer. In the realm of the absolute, there is simply oneness; both the question and the answer become one and what exists is only the presence of their union. To acquire knowledge, to indulge in desires and to experience life as it unravels, our consciousness attaches itself to dualities in dichotomies. Thus, we realize the meaning of life.

***

The mind separates the absolute energy at its two extremities and stretches it in order to gain knowledge and choose the better option of the two. Without separating the subject from its subject-object relationship in oneness, how will the knower (self-subject) through knowing (mind) gain knowledge about any particular field or object? Therefore, the meaning of life can be experienced and realized by the mind only by separating the presence of its being (awareness) into dual living, culminating in those experiences to form what is called consciousness.

Such a development allows the consciousness to expand, evolve and transform in order to make its own individuality. For that matter, even physical existence is a constant adjustment between two poles: the inhalation and exhalation of the breath. Without one the other does not exist. *Therefore, the greatest paradox of life is that all opposites are actually not two but one.*

***

The cycle of birth and death by itself is a paradox. Both are different and yet one; both come from nothing and go back into that nothing or the absolute. According to Hindu beliefs, death is nothing but the beginning of a new birth.

We may presume there is a difference between male and female, but that difference also is a duality of the same energy in a relative reality that is apparent and paradoxical. Both, in fact, constitute a single energy in continuum, but in different forms, existing in their polarities for a limited period. Both remain separated, but become one during sex, for this form of energy to be created further.

This is how energy expands and grows and separates into its opposites with the poles disengaged, but yet remains within that absolute, as part of the same whole. When opposites conjoin, there is synthesis and expansion takes place. Growth never stops because synthesized energy again separates into its own fields to remain alive and this can happen only by disjoining.

There would be no life on this earth if the absolute energy did not separate into its duality; evolution would come to a stop simply because energy in its absoluteness is static and dormant. It is like positive and negative in the form of electrical energy; like charges repel and opposites attract, creating an electric field. Absolute energy remains constant and defines each and every form as parts of the same whole to exist temporarily within its own ultimate reality. In that wholeness of one, different forms with their respective characteristics emerge within the same energy to come and go. Eventually, what remains is that formless, fundamental absolute energy.

***

We as humans have been blessed with the power of choice. This is also a paradox because choice can be both: a blessing as well as a curse. Choice has a tendency to create conflicts and also prove to be materialistically beneficial, since we always choose the best out of any two in our self-interest. We basically choose to accumulate wealth and material possessions hoping this will give us everlasting happiness, health and comforts. The more we have, the higher are the conflicts within us and the feeling of insecurity persists. Even if all our wants are fulfilled, so long as we separate the oneness of any energy into two and choose one, conflicts will remain.

***

The human mind, because of its duality, is never satisfied and it is never certain about anything. Alternatives always remain open and this is the cause of conflict. Our perceptions become illusory as we, driven by greed, amass more and more, leading to fear (that we will lose everything) and, eventually, to gradual disintegration of our life. Today, we buy more, but enjoy less. We have bigger houses with smaller families; more knowledge but less wisdom; and more medicines yet less wellness. We have the technology to save time in everything we do, but still are always short of time. We *fall* in love, but do not know how to *rise* in love.

Now, suppose we gradually reduce our desires and wants while existing in such dichotomies and become less judgemental. Suppose we become a little more spontaneous and proactive, instead of being calculating and reactive, always differentiating between what is good or bad, beautiful or ugly, and think of them as one, just as nature has meant them to be. Suppose we learn how to accept both happiness and sadness as one, with grace and awareness. Then we would be in unison with nature and we would achieve a certain balance between the material and the spiritual. We would move closer towards that absoluteness with oneness existentially, where paradoxes are reduced and reality shines. Both are essential; it is realizing that correct balance between the two, which can make our lives more fulfilling.

***

The lotus flower emerges from the dirty water of a pond or river, yet remains aloof, detached and pure. In spirituality, the lotus flower represents the ability not to attach oneself, in spite of being surrounded with desires. It lives with ease in dirty water and is a symbol for spiritual growth in purity and transcendence. In order to sustain life, both fields are required, as long as we know how to use our mind and not be used by it. This knowledge will take us closer towards the immense beauty of nature, which provides abundant forms of energies, from sexual to divine, so long as we know how to create in unification and not suffer due to conflicts in separation.

***

In this concrete world of ours, with most of us having egocentric minds, we need to be alert and aware; otherwise we are bound to deplete our energies becoming mentally and physically weak. Spirituality believes that even if we shall eventually decay, we should lead a complete and wholesome life in which there is capital, comfort, contentment and compassion. We should not be indifferent to any of these entities; all are needed for us to experience fulfilment in totality. We may not realize the equilibrium in oneness of the absolute, but moving towards it shall bring us joy and peace of mind.

***

As Plato,* the great Greek philosopher, said: 'I am the wisest man alive for I know one thing and that is that I know nothing.' Even contradictory statements can reveal the truth if it is looked upon not logically but existentially. The deeper we enter the inner self, accompanied by self-knowledge with self-awareness in self-experience, the more will we realize the wisdom behind the secrets of existential living with nothing in the mind.

***

Throughout our life, we are seeking happiness in one form or another, narrowing it down selfishly to only being happy when we get what we want, otherwise not. Existentially, happiness is not something that we may seek; it should be in our basic nature. The more we pursue happiness, the higher will be the agitation, anxiety and apprehension with sadness following like a shadow.

If we cannot be happy just as we are, we will never be happy. We will always think of one condition or another to be happy. We should not seek happiness in the future; instead, we should be happy existentially in 'the now'.

---

*Plato: 428/427 or 424/423 B.C. to 348/347 B.C.

Happiness is a way of life. The paradox arises simply because we presume that both dual characters exist as two separate entities. In reality, it is the absence of one for a short while that creates the emergence of the other. It is in the absence of happiness that sadness appears; both are, in fact, one in their absolute nature.

***

Life is constantly in motion, separating into dualities and relating to opposites. People who are lonely complain about silence and lack of companionship and those who love their own company discover bliss in aloneness with nature. As mentioned in the epigraph to this chapter, countless people die every day, yet we dream of living forever. The list of desires is seemingly endless and the words to describe them are few and inadequate; it is only in existential living when words cannot define life's experiences, realization creates inner wisdom within us.

The road to inner freedom cannot be found in words or by making efforts. Our true nature manifests itself in the presence of our being with awareness, from one moment to the next. Inner peace is always in abundance, being the infinite timeless and formless spirit. We keep seeking inner peace through books, teachers and other sources (say, the Internet), not realizing that what exists is only one single entity. All dichotomies are but two sides of the same coin.

Therefore the awareness, which I keep repeating time and again, makes us aware of how to balance the various flows of energies operating within us. It also makes our mind conscious, while experiencing those polarities of existence as to why we should accept both with equal grace and respect. Both happiness and sadness, in fact, are a part of the same absolute. Once we become aware of them, as and when they appear and accept them gracefully, we will not get easily excited, agitated or disturbed with either pleasure or pain. Life then becomes a celebration for us to experience and realize its true nature.

***

All that we seek is within us. During the initial stage of our life, seeking knowledge is a must; after that we only need to experience life and realize it with that ever-flowing intense state of awareness. When the seeker (in awareness) seeking (through the mind) becomes one with the seen (the object), all paradoxes vanish and what remains is absoluteness in total silence. The divine nature residing within us cannot be described by any philosophical or scientific concept except by our own experiences of godliness in love and compassion in life.

Chapter 20

THE POWER OF THE SPIRIT

You have to grow from the inside out. None can teach you, none can make you spiritual. There is no other teacher but your own soul.

— Swami Vivekananda

What is the power of the spirit? It is that absolute field of conscious energy in the form of awareness within the mind performing as a witness, which is considered the presence of 'who' we are. It provides us with the insight of knowing beyond our five senses about the physical world. It is the presence of our being, the state of our mind, which connects us to one another. We are all endowed with different levels of spiritual, psychic and physical fields of energy. It is these fields from which we have the ability to evolve and transform the energy into something that we call our uniqueness or individuality.

***

Though the West coined the word 'spirit' much later, we, however, are referring to that spirit what the Upanishads of ancient India called 'Brahma' or 'Brahman'. It comes from the Sanskrit root '*brh*', which means to expand, and the ending letters denote what is finally formed. It refers to the absolute concept central to Hindu philosophy concluding 'Brahmand' as the universe, which, in spite of internally growing and continuously expanding, still remains constant, indivisible and intact.

The fundamental message of the Upanishads is that this Supreme spirit is present in every single aspect of this universe, from the subatomic particles to the planets and we are also a manifest part of the same, in a relative form. On its own, it remains changeless and not aware of itself. However, within its own infinite self, it keeps manifesting in different forms, changing and expanding from one source of aware spirit/energy into another. Hence, this concept comprises the unchanging or unmanifest wholeness of the absolute spirit containing and also comprising the continuous changing transient manifestation but remaining in totality as one and the same. Both are part of the one and only Supreme spirit.

I repeat: at one end we have the manifest and, at the other, the unmanifest; both being indivisible even though separated from each other, continue to remain within the same totality in the wholeness of their oneness. These two can separate for a limited time, but cannot be divided. We as human beings are endowed with the ability to express both aspects, the manifest as the body/mind and the unmanifest as the absolute aware energy, being that witnessing self, residing within. The essence of this principle is that life should be lived in totality within its own oneness in a wholesome manner. However, the mind, in order to grow and expand, requires separation to choose between this and that, which, in turn, creates a constant struggle between the absolute unchanging spirit and the relative format of the continuously changing body and mind.

Therefore, the relative forms of the body-mind keep changing, and the witness, the spirit continues to watch as that absolute, remaining unchanged. The relative and the absolute flow in their own ways; the body-mind constantly desires for separation in self-interest and the spirit, on the other hand, demands that wholeness in totality. Both need to be experienced and we are required to discover the presence of this absolute unchanging spirit from within the constantly changing body and mind.

The art of life is that the relative knowingly needs to experience life as the relative. This is in order to expand, evolve and transform with the aid of that knowing spirit of absolute awareness, which makes our mind aware and conscious enabling us to know our true reality of who and what we actually are.

***

The spirit is that subject of the centralized absolute power that, as per its individual intensity, structures our mind/consciousness to perform either in favour of the material self in selfishness or in favour of the divine towards selflessness. When anything stimulates our body or mind; we visualize, focus on and synchronize with that object of interest and initiate moves to become aware and conscious of it (the object). Our inner power then broadens a certain field of consciousness for us to experience what life is all about.

***

An animal can be aware to perceive any situation but cannot become conscious of itself to conceptualize it. The animal may watch the scene around it for a while and may focus on a prey and even catch it, but will not develop its intellect or create something new. In this sphere, the human mind is superior; we become conscious to conceptualize what we are aware of. We can also understand, experience and analyse our concepts apart from being able to measure things quantitatively and qualitatively dissecting everything minutely. Not only that, our mind also has this ability to become aware of its own mind functioning in awareness.

Moreover, we are those unique living creatures that become conscious to also ignite the intellect to study any object or situation of interest. The power of the intellect, through reasoning and choice, draws certain inferences from what it conceives within its own limitations of memory and emotions.

***

The essence of spiritual recognition and consistency in whatever we perceive is revealed only if we are *consciously aware of our own self*. Aware energy is that absolute cosmic spirit, which manifests itself in our mind and is the fundamental cause for attaining everything. It is that primordial spiritual power, which takes the mind beyond sensory perceptions into perceiving the unknown intuitively and creatively, but spontaneously without analysing and dissecting. It is unconditionally free, independent and self-sustaining, dealing with areas of consciousness beyond the limits of personal identity. It is the ground of our being and is that power, which makes us who we are; in fact, it is the presence of our spiritual being.

***

Spiritualism considers the cognitive mind as the illusory self and the degree of individual aware energy as the true Self. It is the real Self, being the witnessing mind, which is responsible for making the mind aware and become conscious, in order to indulge in, and experience, what it chooses, intends and infers. The series of experiences, which the physical mind goes through in self-consciousness, evolves and transforms, making us realize that we are all spiritually one. This realization of who and what we are becomes the subject and practice of spirituality. The spiritual power of awareness becomes the subject in which the mind is the object of its aliveness or consciousness.

The cognitive mind basically is comprised only of thoughts. Nevertheless, all of us would admit there is nothing greater than thoughts. Why? Life is centred around, and expresses itself, through thoughts. However, if we are mentally victimized or tortured by negative thoughts, then the mind turns into an inferno.

The mind, which is supposed to be our tool, becomes our master and results in controlling us through improper conditioning, rigidities and blind beliefs resulting in a state of fear, anxiety and suffering. Consequently, the mind functions through such unconscious thoughts and beliefs by imitating other people, thereby killing our own personal power and intuitiveness. This is where the inner vision of spiritualism comes in handy. We can learn the methods of meditation with complete awareness to attain joy and peace of mind.

***

What is the power of the spirit? The absolute cosmic energy, when manifesting itself within the mind, becomes aware to make it (the mind) conscious in order to experience life. It awakens us to this fact that the personal and the impersonal, the manifest and the unmanifest, the changing and the unchanging, the seen and the unseen, the God and the devil, the absolute and the relative, the time and the timelessness all represent zero in their absoluteness of oneness. Meaning until and unless the material and the spiritual merge back to their point of zero in oneness, there will be no solace. We should not separate the two, as they are one.

The inner is the spiritual and the outer the mental. Whether our mind agrees to this or not does not change its reality. We do not need beards, turbans or saffron clothes to show us this togetherness. Nor do we need any prefixes or suffixes attached to our names to declare our spiritual proficiency. What we need is to self-discover this power on our own. What we actually need is that suffix of '*ness*' denoting the power of that individual aware energy, the aware-*ness*, which reveals the intensity of our conscious aware self.

The spiritualist is ignorant, so is a mentalist, as long as they remain separate. They are not aware that our individual name, fame and knowledge have no spiritual meaning, unless we dissolve with all as one to become aware and conscious, experience to realize this whole as one and not two.

***

In spiritualism, the spirit is that absolute non-dual witnessing Self in total awareness, perceiving, experiencing and realizing what life is all about. It is our mind, which plays the primary role of carving a unique individuality in each and every person, through its own degree of awareness. We can only experience what conforms to our mind through its level of awareness in each individual. This indicates that we are a part of that infinite total awareness, called soul, guiding us how to evolve and transform ourselves in the course of our life.

In the spiritual connotation, the witnessing Self is separate from the evolving self-consciousness or body/ego consciousness. In order to be at par with the unified cosmic consciousness or the soul, first we need to experience and realize its purity in total awareness. This concept of self-realization in pure consciousness has been elaborated upon in many chapters, since awareness and consciousness form the central axis on which the study of spiritualism is based.

***

The mind conceptualizes everything, evolving through space and time; both factors are deeply interconnected. It is through time that thinking expands and continues, but sustains its illusory sense of self-identification. It creates a sense of separation, going away from the centre of its oneness. Spiritual awareness is heightened when the mind is focused on the present moment in mindfulness and does not brood about the past or the future.

The five senses limit physical awareness and encourage undisciplined thoughts, chattering here and there, thus distracting us from the psychic awareness of the present moment. They simply work on auto-mode deriving information from the subconscious. These thoughts are often misleading, since they are emotional and biased activating a strong need for that inner awareness to work in a conscious manner. This is where the power of spirituality takes over, empowering the mind with tantra (meditative methods in higher consciousness) combined with mantra (meditative chanting sounds) and yantra (geometrical calculations to absorb extra energy). It reveals how to make the spiritual energy flow freely and intensively.

As stated earlier, the mind chooses what it desires mainly in self-interest, which creates desires for affluence and material possessions, limiting the mind to only ego in self-identification. In such a situation, the mind oscillates between the material and the spiritual, with limitations in the former and liberation in the latter. Chattering of thoughts, besides desires to attachments, restricts the mind, which can remain balanced and unrestricted only through spiritual power. Both are essential for our personal evolution: one for material existence and the other for spiritual empowerment in surrendering the ego and accepting all that unfolds with the passage of time.

Therefore, it is our mind, which ultimately chooses the path – physical, intellectual, emotional or spiritual or a balance of all of them. This decision and its evolvement are based on our self-awareness in self-experience, creating self-consciousness. Inner transformation can only be self-realized by experiencing the truth by us. This flowering of life through our consciousness, ultimately, is responsible for determining our individuality, enabling us to realize who and what we are. We should remember that consciousness couldn't exist without the perceiver (the subject in awareness) perceiving (through the mind) the perceived (the object in hand) to experience and realize that, which is reality.

***

The dance of the cosmos that we see and observe is simply a play of the aforementioned reality, which the mind has to watch and experience. It can choose either or both: the dual living in the physical space and time or the existential living in the reality of 'the now', meaning the absolute and the relative. The process of spirituality commences with awareness being the focal point. We transcend physicality or the objective self, effortlessly moving into the subjective or the spiritual Self.

Therefore, everything that we conceive and perceive is attributed only to the mind. We may think that our mind is free to choose from various options and decide on its own. However, when we witness our own mind, we realize that it is largely conditioned by the beliefs and thoughts it contains, thanks to our parents, teachers, friends and preachers. Therefore, if we are not careful, our mind keeps imitating everything (like a parrot) what has been downloaded from others, not even being aware of the same.

***

The power of the cognitive mind remains restricted to the limited field of belief in objectivity. However, when it becomes spiritually aware, moment to moment, through alert observation and watchfulness, it connects with the subject of life. It is that subject, which emerges from the infinite space of probability into its actuality of that existential 'now'. In spirituality, this is referred to as 'mindfulness'. We enter the realm of spontaneous awareness in creativity and intuition, rather than being obsessed with the past or the future. The thinking mind may be restricted in its objectivity. However, when it observes with awareness, it merges with the limitless energy all around, bringing us into the reality of our existence, in the present moment, per se.

***

We should never forget that the human mind is the ultimate machine of nature, a complex network of neurons in a blaze of electromagnetic and neural-chemical activity. It is the sovereign holder of spiritual awareness, overseeing and expressing all the experiences we go through in life. Thoughts reflect our deep-seated beliefs about who and what we are or what the world is all about. It is strictly not a part of the body since it has no form or shape; it is basically a processor, which just knows by the intensity of its aware conscious energy. The problems surface when we identify ourselves, separating the absolute, by becoming attached to our emotions and desires, into this or that. This separation from the oneness of the absolute is the cause and suffering of all our misery and sadness.

The energies from awareness, consciousness and the intellect all manifest themselves within the mind to interact and create new ideas, visions and images. In the words of the Buddha: 'All things are preceded by the mind, led by the mind [and] created by the mind.'

***

I have been repeatedly saying that the mind can either be a friend or a foe depending on the use we put it to. It is for us to choose; either in the existential reality of our presence in awareness or in the drift towards emotions of the past with wants in the future. If we fill the mind with negative thoughts, life becomes a burden. All achievements seem beyond reach, magnifying the stresses of daily living. If, on the other hand, we fill the mind with positive thoughts and act upon the same, life will become happier and less stressful. We should try to focus inwards and reap the rewards, simply by watching in mindfulness, through our spiritual mind.

Chapter 21

WHAT IS THE SOUL: 1?

The soul neither lives nor dies.
The soul is neither your body nor mind.
The soul can neither be created nor destroyed.
The soul, forever, dances in awareness.
Be conscious to experience and realize.
What this soul is all about.

— Gian Kumar

What is a soul? Nobody can answer this question with certainty and conviction and with proof. Scientifically, there is no such thing as a soul. Spiritually, the soul is our innermost essence of who and what we are. It is that 'I', which resides in the body and oversees our existence. It is that immaterial part of our body, which is considered to be immortal, transmigrating into another body after death.

The supreme intelligence energy is that God within, which guides the mind and represents itself as the core energy. The mind and body, being the subtle and gross, respectively, expand, evolve and transform to experience life and realize its beauty. In abstract terms, the role of the soul is more like that of a heart within the mind.

***

Spiritual theories claim that the moment the soul attaches itself to a human body, it separates into two. The first is the divine performing as the witnessing self, which is the foundation of our being, where it remains as pure consciousness in total awareness. The second relates to the soul's dual living. Here, it behaves as the individual self, expanding and evolving with self-consciousness to experience the relativities of existence, with desires and attachments due to ego.

In the former situation, the *soul* behaves as the *soul* and, in the latter, as the spirit with primordial awareness, for the sake of the illusory self, forming our inner consciousness. This inner spirit also develops and forms our unique individuality within that aware self. The consciousness or spirit keeps evolving until it realizes the purity of that witnessing Self in total awareness to be at par with the soul.

To further elucidate, the individual witnessing soul is basically a part of that web of universal consciousness, complete and finished in all respects. It continues to live on by declaring that each one of us exists with both as one unit. The soul represents the force of energy with the inner evolving spirit representing it as its field. This source of aware energy keeps on revolving in various cycles of birth and death searching for its destination. It wishes to rejoin its unified force after it has been fully transformed in seeking its purpose in life. The soul is considered to be in that finished stage of the Absolute Self with pure consciousness in total awareness.

***

Ancient Eastern philosophy explains that consciousness is that spirit, which gradually expands and evolves through experiences in any individual, depending on its degree of awareness. In the human body, it expands from the child to ego consciousness besides undergoing a transcendental journey for experiencing to realize its destination in purity. Evolving in this manner, the unfinished spirit continues to transmigrate through multiple cycles of birth and death, until it reaches that finished stage of its purity, referred to as self-realization.

This theory is based upon 'Ishvara' a concept, which means that each one of us is 'capable of' ultimately cognating and existing as equal to that of the Supreme Being, whom we refer to as God.

***

We have three theories in spiritualism clarifying what the spirit or the soul is all about.

The first theory is related to religion. According to Wikipedia: '... the mainstream of Christianity, the *Holy Spirit,* is one of the three divine persons of the *Holy Trinity*, who make up the single substance of God; that is, the Spirit is considered to act in concert with and share an essential nature with God the Father and God the Son (Jesus).'

For Hindus, all that exists are manifestations of God, whereas Islam believes that all that exists is divine creation, rather than divinity itself, meaning that everything belongs to God.

The second theory refers to that ability in each one of us to transform our consciousness. We become capable of synthesizing our soul going through multiple cycles of birth and death, until we self-realize with the Supreme Being.

The third theory, which my books are all about, refers to that highest universal principle declared during the prehistoric times: the ultimate reality as the Para-Brahman (the highest Brahman). This theory is directed towards that ultimate absolute ingredient, which exists in oneness in a unified scheme of the universe. It is an intelligent design where all that exists is one and not two and within the confines of which everything emerges and dissolves back into that same oneness. This absolute spirit is that fundamental ingredient, which binds everything in the universe as one complete whole, without involving any preceptor (God).

The third theory becomes relevant when we consider all three forms of energies – body, mind and spirit (soul) – as one ultimate ingredient. According to this theory, the spirit and matter are interchangeable and not to be regarded as separate entities. Everything depends upon the permutation and combination of gases, liquids and solids combining together within it to destroy and create distinct forms of energies. Within this absolute, all forms exist and express their own attributes and disintegrate to go back into the same. On its own, the absolute remains constant, eternal, limitless and infinite, comprising the whole universe as one single entity.

It is within this concept of non-dualism that the theory of dualism emerges but soon dissipates. In physics, the laws of quantum mechanics and those of thermodynamics have been inspired by this very concept of Para-Brahman.

***

The spiritual message relayed by the spirit in the third theory is very simple. The supreme absolute law of the universe neither blesses nor punishes any of its forms. It only responds to the vibrations in different frequencies, whether positive or negative, in the same manner that we think, perceive and act.

***

Let us now find out how some of the top spiritual maestros have described the complex phenomenon (or the soul) to the famous US TV personality Oprah Winfrey in different episodes on Super Soul Sunday (December 2012):

- GARY ZUKAV: The soul is that part of you that existed before you were born and that will exist after you die. It's the highest, most noble part of yourself that you can reach for.
- ECKHART TOLLE: The soul is your innermost being, the presence that you are beyond form. The consciousness that you are beyond form, that is the soul. That is who you are in essence.
- DEEPAK CHOPRA: The soul is the core of your being. It is eternal. It doesn't exist in space/time. It's a field of infinite possibilities, infinite creativity. It's your internal reference point with which you should always be in touch.
- WAYNE W. DYER: The soul is the birthless, deathless, changeless part of us. The part of us that looks out from behind our eyes and has no form. The soul is infinite so there is no in or out of it. It is everywhere. There's no place that it is not.

Therefore, a human soul is the personification of existence. The way we have a mind and a body, we do not have a soul, because we are that soul. The soul is that core energy where the body represents gross energy and the mind subtle energy. The difference between the spirit and the soul is that the former performs in the initial stages of experiencing duality within the primordial awareness in self-consciousness. This stage is directly proportionate to the quality of the awareness within any human existence.

When we observe our mind spiritually, we find that our mind has separated this absolute energy into a duality. One part of this duality belongs to the ego; the other remains intact, guiding the former by witnessing what it is doing. The absolute part of the mind, since it carries the experience of all humankind, is the soul. It is the identity of who we are as the eternal absolute spirit, fully realized in all respects. It is the divine, residing within as the witnessing self: 'Thou art that.'

***

Our ego mind may be knowledgeable, but it has yet to experience and realize that divinity within. It is that inner spirit consumed with self-identification seeking to return to its core. In order to experience it has to relate everything to its opposite, constantly changing in duality to realize what it desires, choosing among various options in self-interest.

The job of the mind is to be alert and aware in order to make it conscious of what dual living is all about to indulge in and experience. Spiritually, when our mind and body are controlled by the ego, resulting in attachments and desires, it is considered to be ignorant or partially conscious. Any individual presuming the body and the mind to be the real self exists with a false impression of his own self and is separated from the oneness of its absolute nature. Existence, in such a case, revolves with duality and relating in opposites around mental images of what the sensory organs perceive in illusions falsely considering them to be real.

I repeat: the soul is described as the core or the source of the aware field of energy in any human being. It becomes the subjective force, which guides the objective field of the mind and the body consciousness. It serves as the guiding force, witnessing the mind and body, until self-consciousness fully realizes its actual potential.

The soul is also referred to as the 'experiencer', because it is the series of experiences in existence, which leads us to mature and awaken from the ignorance that we are not just body and mind but something beyond. Knowledge, in the spiritual context, is considered to be the dark side of the ego, unless accompanied by experiential realization, which leads one to wisdom. Therefore, in the study of spiritualism, it becomes necessary that an individual recognize that journey of the soul in experiencing the nature of the higher self.

What is more interesting is why is this 'experiencer' considered as the divine within? This is simply because God is not to be found in churches or temples or other religious places; He resides within us as the real absolute Self. God reveals Himself only when we undergo the experiences in divinity. God is purely the presence of any divine experience, which we may realize through our acts of selflessness, and that too, only in oneness with that absolute.

***

Through ages of conditioning by various obscure interpretations, the mind gets entrapped in hope, faith and blind belief, wrongly forming an external image; God is our saviour, whom we should revere. He alone can absolve us from all suffering. We keep on searching outside for that God, our Creator, an external form existing outside, more out of fear rather than out of love. We are unable to comprehend that we are supposed to discover God or the soul from within our inner experiences living with selflessness, compassion and fearlessness.

Theoretically, we may feel good to read about an individual soul or consciousness returning to its source in search of self-realization. Furthermore, it goes through multiple existences of birth and death until it attains self-realization in the ultimate form of the absolute to return to the unified field of consciousness after liberation, moksha, nirvana and so on. However, the same can be questioned with respect to the rationality of this stage: whether transmigrating back into its source to reappear once again in a new birth is possible in our physical, materialistic existential state or not.

The absolute, in reality, exists in a dormant state in the form of dark energy as nothing, which, by its own self, is changeless, limitless and infinite. It is inactive, until it goes into motion and changes from the formless into a form; the infinite into the finite; and the spirit into matter, interchangeable, but retaining its real identity as that of the absolute.

In the finite stage, consciousness is active and attaches itself to duality within space, time and matter. However, after death, it again merges back with that dark space, which is latent and nothing. To consider that as the unified field of aware consciousness is more of a wild guess. It originates more out of belief, faith and opinion, which one cannot challenge.

Moreover, a field of energy, after leaving its force disperses in entropy and randomness, never to return to its source. For instance, the Sun emits light and heat as energy, which never returns to the source.

In today's world, with an ever-increasing human population, one wonders on the efficacy of how an individual consciousness can return intact to a new birth; all calculations are bound to go haywire.

How an individual soul can transmigrate, with all its unfulfilled desires, to carry on in its next birth to attain completeness remains in doubt. Yes! One thing is certain, there is no end to life, and it is always a beginning from one birth to another, from the absolute to dual existence and back into the absolute. The total amount of energy remains constant and only changes its form, from one into another, expanding and evolving within the totality of its infinite existence.

***

The basic truth of spiritualism revealed by our ancient sages, I suppose, was mainly to point towards a guiding factor in that oneness of our absolute energy, the existence of the one and only nature of our ultimate reality. However, separate nomenclatures were created by different teachers in due course of time, wherein concepts of I-Amness, Beingness, Consciousness, Total Awareness and Self were to indicate the presence of the state of the Absolute. Our job primarily is to expand our consciousness, transcending into a higher spiritual realm by methods of experiential living referred today as spirituality.

To a mystic, it becomes difficult to define in words what a soul is, unless he goes into the mythical and religious aspects of consciousness. Science may or may not agree, but most scientists do accept that they have a consciousness ruling their mind. Moreover, most of them also visualize there is something beyond for them to delve deeper into the secrets of our universe. People like me, who rely more on reason and logic, being rational and pragmatic, try to express and answer the complexities of life and soul in a commonsensical manner.

Spirituality, the practice of spiritualism in the form of tantra and yoga, firmly believes in the existence of an individual soul, not bothering whether it transmigrates from past regression into afterlife. It does not refer to any

God or religion. Science, on the other hand, will always doubt the existence of an individual soul unless proven; it delves more into the objectivity of any subject rather than the subject itself. Therefore, it considers the soul mystical and mysterious, never realizing that it is purely a series of inner experiences provided to all living creatures varying from one to another.

The day science is able to measure and infer what an experience is all about, probably consciousness will then become a known fact and not a belief. Furthermore, in the case of consciousness it becomes more complicated because it behaves as the absolute Self and also the dual small self simultaneously. In ego consciousness, it exists by experiencing dualities, evolving and transforming, and, in purity, retains its divine identity.

Similarly, science too has experienced the same behaviour in its observations. We have the dual nature of any subatomic particle exhibiting, simultaneously and separately, both properties of a wave and a particle flashing here and there. When observed under an ultrapowerful microscope, these waves and particles become visible. We simply cannot measure them separately as they are, in actuality, one and not two.

Chapter 22

WHAT IS THE SOUL? 2

A Buddha is a Buddha, a Krishna is a Krishna, and you are you. And you are not in any way less than anybody else. Respect yourself, respect your own inner voice and follow it.

— Osho

Today, we often use the words mind, soul and spirit interchangeably as and when we wish, having only a cursory idea of what our ancient sages and religious and spiritual masters meant about their nature and function. The interpretations too, as time went by, have been varied and newer theories keep on getting introduced. We should also keep in mind that what was narrated during the ancient days was as per the circumstances prevailing at that time, which are far different from today.

I have already explained in the previous chapter in great detail about the diverse aspects of the soul. Today, most religious and spiritual masters are in agreement on the immortality of the soul. There are some who claim that God is the Creator and that the soul lives forever in either heaven or hell. Others say that the soul, after the death of the body, is reincarnated in an endless cycle of birth and death until it self-realizes. Whether we follow faith or logic depends on what our own unique individual mind agrees upon, but not forgetting that the meaning and existence of a soul play a very important part in our lives.

***

First of all, it needs to be pointed out that the existence of the soul cannot be denied, simply for the reason that it is that spirit, which makes us different from all other living creatures. Animals too have a mind with some degree of intelligence, but it is the state of awareness in each one of us, which makes us different from any other creature. It is because of this awareness that we are conscious of our own self and also of all that is around us, while animals are not. It is that immaterial form of energy called spirit, which we bank upon right from the day we become aware of everything, in order to form our consciousness and also for correcting and guiding the mind from the witnessing self in times of need.

However, there are also some of us, who may not deny the existence of a soul, but may reserve our opinion on its immortality factor and its ability to transfer itself into another being for self-realization. We have been regularly told all that exists is one, and if body, mind and spirit are intrinsically one, then every single form of energy constitutes the same absolute. How can anyone be certain whether only the soul existed before birth and transmigrated after its death into another body to exist in its own exclusive form for eternity?

***

All concepts of philosophy, as we know, are merely a construct of the mind until proven. These concepts came into being when sages, according to their culture, environment and personal experiences, and in accordance to the needs of any society during those periods, declared the soul to be that immortal God in order to provide solace and relief from fear, anxiety and suffering.

The cosmic cycle, on its own, remains constant and changeless in its absoluteness; where there is no end, but another beginning of a new cycle. It keeps rotating in its cycle of birth and death, changing from one form into another. The idea of the soul being immortal possibly cropped up from here that it never dies and is presumed to be the solitary absolute. It was not realized that the same absolute ingredient, though different in their forms, subsumes all three, the body, the mind and the soul. According to the cosmic cycle, all are but a part of the same absolute, as the one and only essential reality.

In fact, science also explains the same concept: all that exists remains constant and equal, changing in form but existing as one and only absolute energy. What actually exists in our universe is more of dark energy as nothing, which is latent and untapped. The absolute on its own is nothing and dormant, until it manifests itself in mind as awareness, from which we come to know the presence of this universe and all that exists within its infinite domain.

***

It is finally the mind, which makes the body and the soul aware of all that exists around us. The soul inertly develops as a result of our experiences and reflects our inner personality to those who observe us. It is entirely created by our own acts of experiencing uniquely what life is all about. The phenomenal mind also has an impersonal quotient, which performs as the witnessing self in its absoluteness and is considered to be the presence of that God within.

The personal and the impersonal inner individualities eventually add up to what we call the soul. It is not the soul, but our uniqueness, which remains eternal through our deeds as in the case of the Buddha, Lord Krishna, Jesus Christ, Adolf Hitler, Albert Einstein and many others.

***

In the universe, as mentioned earlier, nothing new is created. The basic ingredient remains the same; it only changes from one form to another: from solids to gases to liquids and back to solids. In the absolute, there is no creation or destruction, but only the beginning of another change in its cycle, say, like in birth and death. These changes keep taking place at random; there is no creator or creation and existence remains just as it is in the absolute sense. Therefore, neither God nor souls are created; we only expand, evolve and transform from the beginning and move from one unique birth into another, where there is no death, but just another beginning.

What we should note here is that since the evolvement of any soul or consciousness is based more upon our experiences than anything else, why should we implicate an outside God as the source of our sufferings due to our own misdeeds? Our past experiences in the form of habits are the sole cause of changes in our own consciousness. We are free enough to decide that if we make mistakes and they bring us misery, we should learn not to repeat them and should transcend from one stage of life to another. We are perfectly capable of rectifying any mistakes on our own and transform ourselves into better human beings. All we need is an alert and aware mind to do so.

Further, we also know for certain that we genetically mutate and transfer our habits and other characteristics, acquired in this life or inherited from our ancestors, from one generation to another. Through heredity, we are connected to our past lives. It is in this life we are meant to evolve further, change for the better from whatever was given to us by our ancestors. Somehow, the above explanation got wrongly construed in making us believe that the changes we undergo are but the transference of our soul from the past to the present and not from genes, which will carry us forward to the next life.

***

The doctrines of the sages were valid during the ancient periods; the masses were then mostly illiterate and ignorant about life and they accepted whatever the wise ones told them. How can we, today, accept the contradiction thrown up by religion, when the preachers declare, on the one hand, that God is within us and, on the other, also, at the same time, ask us to pray to an outside God? The moment we understand and begin to practise spirituality in its true essence, we become certain that the kingdom of God/devil and heaven/hell are all within us, depending upon our very own ideas, thoughts and deeds. There is no need for any religion or spiritualism to convince us on this issue unless we have been blinded by faith.

Today, there is a dichotomy as far as religion is concerned. First, there is a form of religion based on unquestioning loyalty (towards, say, a God or His messenger or a holy book) and the other form believes in compassion and love to be essential for that oneness of all human beings. The former form may be described by different names, but if *some of* its followers go along the path of separation through violence, it is bound to lead only towards terrorism and bloodshed. The latter form will take us towards self-transformation resulting in joy and peace. It is sad that most of us today do not give much consideration towards that divinity in self-transformation with compassion for all.

This is the paramount reason for us to pursue spiritual empowerment by the practice of spirituality. It is all there in our mind; we need not worship a separate God, or seek moksha or nirvana, so long as our thoughts and actions are full of love, compassion, care and understanding for one and all. The *practice* of spirituality should sound the clarion call today; otherwise the reverse (marked by hatred, cruelty and fanaticism) could take place, with alarming consequences for humankind as a whole.

Intellectually, even if we are sound in theoretical spirituality, but do not practise it, we will keep on transforming ourselves into hypocrites. We cannot realize God merely by chanting hymns, praying or reading spiritual/religious books; we can do so only by performing deeds in selflessness and showing compassion towards all humanity.

***

If spiritualism claims that we need to self-realize (especially vis-à-vis the soul), then we had better wake up and transform our experiences into godly ones. We should be true to ourselves and objectively ascertain where we truly stand today. We should also ask ourselves whether or not we feel and care equally for one and all, not through words but through our actions. Or, like most human beings, are we filled with jealousy, contempt and ego, trying to prove that we are superior to others?

***

All religions as well as spiritualism convey in theory the same message: we should be true to our own soul and realize this in truthfulness, both internally and externally. Attending spiritual discourses, chanting our guru's name or praying in temples or churches or other religious places may take us away from our own truth and intensify our ego. Until our religion or guru makes us experience and realize '*who*' we really are, it is of no use. Therefore, we should know the truth about the divinity within with regard to who and what we are and how to realize the purpose of life.

If we are true to, and positive towards, our thoughts, words and deeds, we will come to the realization that theories on religion and philosophy are mere tools for marketing various concepts, which the mind has conceptualized over time. We need to apply our own mind, logic and scientific reasoning to come to a proper answer. All that is required for righteous living is just truth and positivity within our own self. The absolute merely responds to our vibrations and frequencies and to what we inwardly reflect. Spirituality simply focuses on the transmission of vibrating energy in oneness to gain access to that absolute.

Since absolute energy is beyond space and time, existing as dark energy, the dichotomies vis-à-vis duality within non-duality are simply an expression of our understanding the nature of its (the energy's) reality. The absolute exists in 'the now', as it is. All words and concepts can only be made applicable within the physical–mental sphere of our consciousness.

***

In the ultimate state of the absolute, which actually represents nothing and comprises mostly empty space, there is simply no one or anything; there is also no requirement for consciousness to experience anything. We can easily observe that on any avenue, which shows us the expanse of our dark infinite universe.

To comprehend the aforementioned discussion, first we need to truly know our own self, apart from knowing how our mind thinks and acts; after that the essence of living in the present becomes apparent. Existence always remains in the present, but the mind is simply not designed to accept that – it dwells more in the past or in the future. We just cannot exist without the mind, so why not accept the fact that all three will remain in our thoughts – the past, the present and the future. We need to combine them together and live from one moment to the next for our overall well-being.

However, if we are positive in our outlook, our thoughts, words and deeds, irrespective of the time, will create a field by reflecting positivity all around. The past can never be eliminated; it lingers on. And the future cannot be ignored, for we need to think about tomorrow, while living today. Positivity ensures that all three are in consonance, inside and outside, and that our environment and we are suffused with love and compassion. All memories of the past, the dreams of tomorrow and the deeds of today will combine to reward us with peace and joy.

**

Therefore, to be truly spiritual, we need to practise authenticity, sensitivity and positivity. The higher the degree of these three components, the more will be the presence of awareness and its reality within us. Truth and positivity are experiential, absorbing love, reality and God in the absolute oneness of who and what we are. Let us not get into the nitty-gritty of those fancy words in our scriptures, thinking too much about the 'beforelife' and the afterlife and forgetting about how to exist well in this very life.

The process is very simple; if we are true to our own self and control our ego, we can see the positive change in others rather than seeing only their dark sides. The same goes for positivity; if we are positive within, we will just not be able to see the negativity of others. There will be a surge of positive energy flowing, both in and out. The absolute, I keep repeating, simply responds to our vibrations in frequencies that we emit. If it is positive vibrations that we transmit, the same will we receive.

Therefore, with memories of our experiences, we should dream for, and try and achieve, that tomorrow, where an aura of positivity and truth, along with oneness, prevails all around.

A positive attitude exuberantly reflects all that spiritualism teaches; spirituality helps in realizing what the mind undertakes. Truth and positive energy embrace every experience one goes through with awareness, encompassing the concepts given by the mind such as God and devil, soul and body and heaven and hell.

Chapter 23

AWAKENING OF THE SOUL – KUNDALINI

Once the soul awakens, the search begins and you can never go back. From then on, you are inflamed with a special longing that will never again let you linger in the lowlands of complacency and partial fulfillment. The eternal makes you urgent. You are loath to let compromise or the threat of danger hold you back from striving toward the summit of fulfillment.

— John O'Donohue*

Although the previous two chapters have focused in depth on the soul, there is another definition for this entity. The soul is that 'us' in total awareness, with the presence of our being residing inside the body and the mind. Awakening of the soul comprises three stages. It starts by our witnessing our own mind. The second stage comes when we consciously experience the activities of the mind. The third stage arrives when we take full control with complete awareness, dictating to the mind and the body how to function.

*John O'Donohue (1 January 1956 to 4 January 2008) was an Irish author, priest and philosopher.

The first stage leads to becoming aware; the second towards the formation of one's consciousness; and the third to knowing, experiencing and realizing the truth of what the nature of this supreme reality is all about. The details of how to awaken the soul in the first two stages have been extensively discussed in my previous books.*
Given here is an in depth explanation on the meaning and purpose of the third stage.

***

We should note that, in all the three stages, the basic ingredient in the body, the mind and the soul remains the same. The absolute energy, the one and the only essential reality, but varying in forms (being gross in the body, subtle in the mind and core in the soul), functions as one complete unit. In ignorance, the mind, under illusions, presumes that it is separate from the soul and exists in a self-identity of 'me and mine', inviting recurring phases of happiness and sadness. On awakening, the mind experiences and realizes the truth that besides all three being one, the whole universe too exists within the same infinite space of oneness, as the absolute energy in continuum.

***

Science is the study of what can be observed with objectivity in a realistic manner. It takes care of managing the gross energy and the subtle energies, whereas spirituality ensures the overall well-being of the body, the mind and the soul as one entity. Spirituality assists

---

*1. *Know Thyself*, Leadstart Publishing, Mumbai, 2015. 2. *Think from the Heart and Love from the Mind*, Leadstart Publishing, Mumbai, 2015. 3. *The Ultimate Reality*, Leadstart Publishing, Mumbai, 2015.

the inner flow of energy to awaken, enhance itself and transform from separation to unification.

The body and the mind are continuously consuming this energy through thoughts, words and actions. In the process, they lose more energy than they can replenish. Our negative behaviour and actions in our self-interest create inner conflicts and agitations, which deplete a lot of energy. The correct balance of our incoming and outgoing energy is never attained, with the result that we fall victim to sickness, ageing and, finally, death.

Our fundamental energy structure is dependent not only upon inheriting genes from our predecessors but also upon many environmental factors. Today, science is discovering how the microbial genome of bacteria and other species in our body are responsible for maintaining this energy balance. Mental imbalances too play a large role in such depletion. Besides recharging our energies through food, exercises, meditation and so on, our ancient sages had devised other measures to channelize surplus energy in order to awaken our body, mind and soul and lead them towards higher consciousness.

They noticed an abundance of primal sexual energy lying dormant or being wasted, especially after the completion of the reproductive requirements. Methods were devised to transfer this powerful energy upwards, in order to awaken the mind and take it to a state of elevated consciousness. In this manner the dormant energy based in the lower spine, instead of being allowed to leak here and there in wasteful thoughts and actions, was used for one's spiritual uplift.

Just imagine the time, energy and effort we waste in sexual thoughts or in adultery, which can otherwise be utilized for higher purposes. Most of us would agree that if this dormant energy could be made available for better purposes, it would be of great help in ensuring our well-being. All that is required are proper thoughts and correct methods for transferring this energy for the channelling of our consciousness into righteous activities. The ancient sages devised methods from mantra (sounds to aid meditation), tantra (meditative methods in higher consciousness) and yantra (geometrical calculations to absorb extra energy), which are in great demand today in the belief that they can lead us from the realm of sex to superconsciousness.

***

When science investigates the human body physiologically and psychologically, it concentrates mainly on the physicality of any individual being. However, spirituality, after knowing the truth of its own real self, applies methods of mantra, tantra and yantra with the aid of yoga (plus mindfulness) to increase the flow of inner energies for attaining superconsciousness.

If we are serious about achieving any spiritual progress, we must first learn, understand, and experience life to realize the basic aware inner energy flowing through the body and the mind from our primordial intuitive and innate awareness. However, when we reach a higher state in spirituality; we discover the presence of non-active energy lying untapped, situated at the base of the spine, which can easily be utilized for good deeds. This latent energy is called 'kundalini' and, if aroused, transports the soul to a higher dimension of spiritual wisdom. This vortex of primal energy, as described, is located in a serpent-like manner at the base of the coccyx, lying dormant, yet to realize its true potential.

Kundalini has a direct connect with the human brain. When we are sexually aroused, both the mind and the sexual organs become attached as one. Without the mind, it becomes difficult to function in sex. The energy between the two entities, psychic as well as physical, moves in a spiral-like pattern via the spine, with energetic blood rushing into the lower area in order to perform any sexual act. There is a tremendous flow of mental, physical and emotional energy, which is utilized to bring forth the continuity in life.

The negative aspects emerge when the mind remains obsessed with sex in the form of lewd thoughts and images, thereby depleting energy through lust and desire. The moment one human being views another with lust, he or she gets carried away and indulges in regrettable activities. Such sort of sexual cravings also enhance further the desire for material things. The prime energy starts leaking all around without any sensible purpose. We should keep in mind that besides the significance of the breath, sexual energy is also considered to be prime, since it signifies the beginning of a new cycle of life.

When one realizes the serious impact of wasting such vital energy, a spiritual demand arises to transmute, transfer and transcend the same. The energy here is shifted from the root chakra to the crown chakra, where the mind connects with the cosmos. We become aware that everything occurring in our mind is simply the manifestation through conditioning of our thoughts culminating in subconscious beliefs. At that moment, we long to awaken our true self; but only after knowing and experiencing life along with knowledge does the transformation begin, and that is when meditation becomes a reality. We reach a pure stage of intense awareness of all that is around us, devoid of psychic or sexual desires.

***

The power of the kundalini remains dormant in all of us, like a coiled serpent, asleep, waiting to be awakened to display its power. This is the ultimate spiritual journey, where the energies flowing from the lower to the higher combine in unison in complete awareness. This combination usually occurs during the later stages of life, when material and bodily needs have been looked after and we transcend into the spiritual zone of what we really are. As mentioned earlier, we are fundamentally spiritual beings going through a human experience. And, when we practise how to combine all the three, body, mind and soul, into one and live that experience, the individual self integrates with the cosmic Self.

***

The soul or, in other words, total awareness, is divine and is the source of divine energy in the form of the kundalini. Kundalini is the esoteric stage of all yoga. Kundalini energy is considered as the divine feminine creative power of Goddess Shakti. This feminine energy is considered to be the foundation of who and what we are. It is represented by its systems of chakras (wheels) coursing spirally upwards, meeting one by one from the root to reach the crown chakra. The union is considered to be the realization of the absolute. The activation of this vital energy enhances ultimate spiritual growth, leading us towards an expanded state of higher consciousness, from the unitary soul towards that unified collective soul. The illumination of this energy is also referred as Chi, Prana or Holy Spirit, which allows the mind to acquire the total awareness to comprehend the oneness, which we all seek.

***

The reason for linking the awakening of the kundalini to sexual energy is because the root or the muladhara chakra is the key where such energy is locked. The journey for transfer of this dispensable energy goes through seven stages, reaching the sahasrara (crown) chakra, which connects us to the cosmos. This is the centre, which, on awakening, makes us experience and realize that we are but an extension of our own consciousness in total awareness and the universe within is no different to the one outside.

When our crown chakra awakens, the soul acquires the intuitive knowledge to balance the physical with the non-physical, accepting all as a part of one, rather than as separate. We should remember that life has only one message for us, whatever anybody may say. It provides us with a unique mind and a body, not just to exist but also to evolve and transform with togetherness for attaining that oneness in understanding the truth and experience in its meaning and the purpose behind each moment.

***

Our intentions and karma determine how we wish to navigate our life, whether in blind beliefs with a conditioned rigid mind or by exercising our own unique personal power. Our deeds, whether positive or negative or whatever our beliefs, have no other option but to act in the service of Mother Nature with humanness and oneness. We need to follow this pattern for the survival of humankind for that macrocosm to continue showering the microcosm with all the benefits that it can provide.

Once we follow this dictum, life in return bestows us with health, wealth and wisdom through awareness. In order to experience the same, sages and seers of the ancient period devised various philosophies, concepts and methods of self-realization, God realization and pure consciousness, through the kundalini, yoga, religion and so on. The intention was to formulate a systematic and orderly passage through life, so that we may be able to comprehend the collective consciousness of who and what we are.

All such concepts were designed to benefit humankind, primarily to serve the purpose of remaining in oneness, which we conveniently tend to forget or ignore. Today, vis-à-vis spirituality, because of gross misunderstanding and lack of practice, these concepts have been virtually reduced to mere theory, breeding hypocrisy by proving our actions to be contrary to our professed noble assertions.

The aforementioned concepts have more or less failed to provide any optimum realization of the purpose of life for humankind. Those who consider themselves authorities in the fields of religion and spirituality should cast aside their desire for propagating their own personalities and their institutions and, instead, merge with the rest of humanity with love and compassion. Until and unless the lesson of a united humankind is imparted with fairness in truthfulness by preachers, gurus, politicians and others, the world will continue to suffer because there can be no real awakening of the soul, which simply cannot survive on its own. Neither will there be any peace as long as we keep trying to outdo and outsmart each other, only for material and worldly gains.

Therefore, the true awakening of the soul happens not through religion or by knowing a wide variety of theories and concepts. It takes place only when any individual soul experiences and realizes in complete awareness that oneness of who and what we are. This process of awakening the kundalini takes place during the third and final stage, primarily for this reason, intensifying our awareness manifold.

***

The soul has been provided with the most phenomenal yantra, a machine called the mind. It has the capacity to manifest the inner energy and the outer passive energy. It converts the latter energy into the active form through awareness, becoming the presence of who we are. It also has the capacity, if directed, to convert surplus energy into our higher consciousness through the kundalini.

The self (or jivatman) has the capacity (through the mind) to utilize both the inner and outer energies in the manner it wishes. It commands the mind either to function in illusions of duality concerning worldly affairs or to lead us towards that absoluteness by being aware of its truth in oneness, where all energies merge into each other in a state of equilibrium.

Chapter 24
Personal Power

Most powerful is he who has himself in his own power.

— Seneca*

Each one of us is unique. We have something special in all of us. It is our own uniqueness, which just cannot be duplicated or compared with anyone else. Personal power is that state of mind, wherein our strength of uniqueness reveals the presence of our individuality. It is the ability to think, feel and reason with our own intensity of aware energy, which gives us the confidence to act in any situation with poise and grace. This ability gives us the power to be in charge of our thoughts and emotions rather than follow or allow others to influence or dictate to us. It is the sum total of our intellect, spirit and will all as one.

Personal power has a direct link to our state of consciousness. As we evolve and become conscious of the inside and outside and take charge, our inner power awakens and reaches a higher state of consciousness. To

---

*Lucius Annaeus Seneca (*circa* 4 B.C. to A.D. 65) was a Roman philosopher and dramatist.

be spiritually conscious means that we are aware of our own self and take responsibility for all our actions, not giving any excuses or providing explanations. Those with a lower state of consciousness normally react negatively to any circumstance, criticize and blame others and are not aware of the nature of their own reality.

***

The role of our conscious mind is basically to provide that ability for correct decision making. On the other hand, the subconscious mind running on auto-mode takes forward both the mind and the body involuntarily in an effortless manner. It is said that over 90 per cent of the mind functions in an unconscious mode, simply because it is faster and the memory is already filled with past awareness to act on its own. In fact, this unconscious portion is a byproduct of the conscious mind and is considered to be more of an illusion. Since it relies more upon past information from its memory, it projects that into the future while missing the essence of the present moment.

***

The moment the mind is awake, it becomes aware and conscious of all that is happening around and also goes further by pre-empting what is about to happen. The conscious mind manages the subjective part where all major decisions are made. The subconscious mind is merely a doer on its own and carries out on various 'errands', depending more upon the behaviour of the individual overly concerned with its self-interest in all that it chooses and decides. Most reflex actions and conditioned reflex actions of the mind do not require consciousness to play their part. This is the reason why the subconscious mind is probably ten times faster when compared to the conscious mind, since the former does not require any duration to be conscious about anything.

The conscious part determines what the mind freshly experiences and the subconscious part does the rest of the routine work, taking care of the numerous other chores and errands.

If a mind makes any mistake in ignorance, it is mainly because of not being conscious of the same. A mind can also become conscious and know things just by seeing, because a seer sees in awareness and not necessarily by thinking. It is thought, which makes the mind deviate from its totality towards separating any object or situation into this or that in order to choose in its self-interest for the sake of self-preservation. This is how the cognitive mind has been designed to think, choose and discern from its sensory perception exclusively for its *'me and mine'*.

Therefore, the three levels of the mind, though scientifically not approved, are widely accepted as a descriptive model to frame the nature of our psychic reality. The *subconscious* consumes the largest part of the mind involving the memory and the intellect. The *conscious* section is primarily restricted to its intensity of aware energy occupying a small portion. The third level is the *unconscious*, which is the deep and unresolved part, simply because of its inaccessibility to connect easily with the conscious and subconscious thoughts.

***

The unconscious part of the mind is devoid of conscious awareness and we have no idea of what data is stored in it. The moment the mind is awake and aware, it becomes conscious and, subsequently, the subconscious takes over.

Therefore, modern psychology is primarily concerned with only two sections of the mind. First, a conscious mind that is free from all bindings and creates new ideas. The second is the subconscious or the supercomputer, which is charged by memory with programmed information automatically reacting by releasing unconscious thoughts.

***

Meditation is all about how to make our mind more conscious, so as to be aware of all that we do in the present moment, rather than our acts being selfishly done subconsciously from the mind's past exhausted awareness.

Results from the conscious mind are more significant and valuable than those from the subconscious mind. It is the spontaneous primordial awareness of any present moment, which makes the mind aware and conscious. And it is those subconscious thoughts, which later draw information from the memory and the intellect via thoughts to form its self-consciousness. It is the conscious level, which 'controls' the mind providing the power to engineer it in accordance with its individual degree of awareness.

In totality, it is the mind's capacity to remember, which makes us experience and realize *who and what* we are. Consciousness, in fact, becomes the *'rememberer'*, drawing its energy from the memory bank and is the sum total of our past experiences. It keeps on expanding and evolving, becoming further aware of what we are. It reveals the degree and quality of awareness in order to transmute and transform within any individual mind.

***

The reason to compare both the conscious and the subconscious is necessary because there are certain scientific discoveries, which are contrary to what is being spiritually claimed. The subconscious may be running our life through unconscious thoughts but the conscious section is what rules, governs and regulates the mind. These discoveries rely more on the objective and quantitative factor of the subconscious, creating an impression to supersede the conscious. The conscious is related more to the subjective and qualitative factor, because it pertains to our unique individual quality of awareness responsible for forming our individuality.

Spiritually, there is no segregation between the conscious and the subconscious, since all that exists is one and not two. The former is the unique nature of one's reality and the latter an illusion created by the mind.

Since conscious thoughts occur purely under awareness, they reflect our inner power to determine the outcome of any situation. When we become conscious of our own presence, apart from being alert and aware that we possess our own personal power, we do not remain a victim of any situation. We thereafter respond to any situation to *proact* spontaneously with an inner strength of awareness rather than *react* emotionally by thinking.

It is these flashes of spontaneous awareness, which are basically devoid of thoughts for a short period that result in creativity and intuitiveness, which our thoughts later recall and put to good use. This is the fundamental essential quality of all successful persons; they exhibit strong personal power, whether in the material world or in the spiritual one, leading to amazing results and shining in all fields of life.

***

The subconscious portion containing the unconscious thoughts of our mind is simply incapable of going inwards to observe and become aware of our own mind, which is the crux of spirituality. How to awaken our consciousness, so that we are able to observe our own mind and its thoughts is the aim of spirituality. In a lower state of consciousness, due to lack of present awareness, we succumb to circumstances, unconsciously allowing them to rule over us. We unnecessarily become a victim of fate or destiny. Emotion and desires cloud our mind and dominate us unconsciously; we are suffused with envy, jealousy, contempt and frustration, boosting a negative self, where we lose all control. We may be conscious of our negative emotions but remain unconscious of the damage they are doing. Our energies get depleted due to a false sense of ego and our attitude becomes pessimistic and unresponsive to all that is happening around us.

***

We can activate and enhance our own personal power, not emotionally, but by going consciously inwards to know the self, observe our own mind and not allow it to go astray. The mind is present in all of us and it is entirely up to us to awaken it, if lying dormant. Many people manage to scale unattainable heights in their lifetime; others struggle unconsciously with daily problems just to survive. Are the former born with superintellect and intelligence? No! It is the personal power in their mind, body and spirit, which makes them consciously undertake the most difficult tasks in life and finish them successfully.

***

Personal power is that inner power, which is directly proportionate to everything that we perceive and become conscious of. It is that determinant of the level of our consciousness, which further determines all our subjective experiences. It ascertains the degree of our awareness, which our mind reveals. The outside world exists, as it is; we just cannot change that, for all experiences are but reflections generated by our own mind. There is really nothing for us to point out, compare, blame or judge in order to suit our own convenience.

What do successful people have in common? It is the ability to draw limitless energy beyond the normal confines of the cognitive mind. They can also tap internally to enhance their own infinite personal power – creative as well as spiritual.

We should awaken and take charge of our consciousness and not allow it to drift. We should empower ourselves spiritually to perceive any negative situation through silent observation. We should proact with aware energy and not emotionally react, becoming conscious and awake in any present moment. We should surrender our ego and accept the situation as it is, and realign our thoughts to act accordingly.

**

Let us now take the case of will power. A person's will is considered to be his capability in making a conscious choice. It is related to desire; the more the desire, the stronger is the force behind that choice. If we do not desire something strongly, the less will be our power towards attaining that goal. That is why we say 'where there is a will, there is a way'. It is more of self-discipline in self-control, an instinct, which comes from both the mind and the body as a reaction to a certain mental action. Will power is utilized more for external reasons rather than transcending that inner self and reaching a higher realm.

During the initial stages, personal power is limited to intellectuality and will power, both responsible for creating our personality. Gradually, as we become aware and conscious of our own mind and our own inner self from its experiences, psychic energies merge both our intellectual and will power into an inner spiritual power. This process eventually culminates in forming the essence of our uniqueness, responsible for possessing a distinct individuality. Therefore, our personality reveals our external image to the world and individuality unveils that uniqueness: the aura of that inner personal power that we possess within.

Allow me to elaborate further. At one end, we have the ego power in the form of our personality and, at the other, there is the personal power of the soul. The former *reacts* to any stimulus after emotionally thinking in self-interest and the latter *proacts* consciously without thinking in spontaneity through observance. In the former, the ego separates the mind's energy into a duality and, in the latter, the energy remains absolute in creative intelligence, until thoughts take over.

The total sum of our personal power eventually forms our individuality, compared to reactive emotions through calculative thoughts that form our 'presumed' personality. In the former, our individuality exudes creativity, openness and sensitivity, responding spontaneously to any stimuli. In the latter, our thoughts manipulate us in order to derive the best results by thinking only in self-interest. Both are required in their own way for the sake of existing in our material and spiritual fields.

***

Individuality is a reflection of our consciousness and personality that of our ego. Individuality, through its spiritual power, liberates us from the clutches of our self-attachments, whereas personality drags us towards materialism.

Individuality, or our personal power, is more of a metamorphosis of our personality. It reveals itself when we rebel against all that has been imposed upon us through blind beliefs in rituals and traditions. When we stop imitating others and experience every action with our own intuitiveness, the process revitalizes our consciousness and helps in changing its direction towards our individuality, our real being. This does not mean that we are against any society, community or organization; our individuality is simply the source of our creativity, flowing out with freshness and freedom.

***

We are not only body and mind, but also the 'experiencer', who reflects upon life either through an egoistic personality or through the spiritual mind, thereby experiencing the self through individuality, that is, intuitively, through personal power. The inner power is the flame of spiritual awareness with our unique personal power, which subsumes ego, thereby indulging in, and experiencing, life through our consciousness. The awareness within us makes us sensitive towards others. Personal power, in fact, is nothing but the degree of our individual awareness, which increases our conscious quotient taking us away from our egoistic self towards the totality.

We monitor events and become conscious after witnessing and then controlling our mind through thoughts and words. We learn how to navigate through our thoughts, emotions and beliefs within the realm of our consciousness. This is that unique power, which gives us the insight that the outside world is not separate, but purely a reflection of our inner consciousness. The world exists as it is; we can neither change it nor do we have any control over it. However, we have limitless power to change our inner self and perceive the outer with a positive view, so long as we are conscious about our actions. In other words, personal power is a reflection of who we are and how we interpret the outside world.

Therefore, we need to raise our consciousness to higher levels, so that we may have enough intrinsic power to promote an outside world in accordance with our expectations and aspirations. This is the key to awakening; we should increase our personal power, so that we are not ignorant, either from the inside or towards the outside world, because both are inherent and intrinsic to each other.

Chapter 25

LIFE ... WHAT A DELUSION!

Most of our difficulties, our hopes, and our worries are empty fantasies. Nothing has ever existed except this moment. That's all there is. That's all we are. Yet most human beings spend 50 to 90 per cent or more of their time in their imagination, living in fantasy.

— Charlotte Joko Beck[*]

It is said that we are lucky to be born as human beings, the only living creatures who are not only aware and conscious of the outside but also are also capable of being conscious of their own 'beingness'. However, we are also those unfortunate creatures who are always complaining and perennially dissatisfied, whether rich or poor. There is a constant feeling of incompleteness in our lives. We feel unfulfilled, without knowing why. We are not happy or content being just as we are.

In Hindu philosophy, the world of duality in which we live is referred to as 'maya' (illusion). Until we achieve victory over our illusory self, whatever we may do or

---

[*]Charlotte Joko Beck (27 March 1917 to 15 June 2011) was an American Zen teacher and author.

achieve, feelings of inadequacy, sorrow and fear will remain. In other words, unless we gain control over our minds, the 'delusion' will persist.

I once heard someone saying that to make substantial progress in our material life, we need to be satisfied by being dissatisfied. The whole process of wanting more and more leads to a paradox, which seems senseless. The search for fulfilling our unending desires keeps us in that vicious cycle of uncertainty, where we constantly revolve in a flux of momentary periods of success and failure and happiness and sadness. We may have all the worldly comforts and luxuries, yet insecurity remains in some form or the other. Most of us come to terms with this state of insecurity, living unconsciously in ignorance, so long as we achieve materialistic comforts in life.

The reason for the acceptance of such insecurity is our unpredictable and unconscious mind, constantly fluctuating due to thoughts, emotions and actions, leading to anxiety and suffering. In spite of enjoying all physical comforts, the dilemma remains. Nature has endowed us with the gift of choice, and choice is what creates conflicts. Animals don't have to use their minds to choose; they decide by instinct. A human being's intellect leads him to select something, analyse it and find out its functions, which he does, mainly for fulfilling his selfish needs. Unfortunately, this kind of living with constant selfishness makes us feel separated from others and insecure. The more we have, the higher is the inner insecurity. The paradox persists and the happiness we seek is never complete.

Moreover, our desires keep changing. What is desirable today may not be so tomorrow. We want to acquire something, soon abandon it and reacquire something else, always wanting more and more. We are torn between our morals and greed or between logic and blind beliefs. A time comes when we wish to get away from all this turbulence and seek peace and tranquillity.

***

Whenever and wherever there is avarice, there shall be suffering, simply because we are opposing what is in the present, the way it is and asking for something in the future. Eventually, we need to control our greed for amassing more and more. We should remember that desire is too strong a dynamic energy, and it shall always remain so. Those who have and the ones who don't, both are unhappy. That is the irony or the delusion of life.

The explanation for such a state of affairs, from a spiritual viewpoint, is rather complex. The mind is designed to separate the absolute energy into its relative duality in order to seek, choose, discern, experience and realize things in self-interest for self-preservation. On the other hand, in order to gain inner peace and tranquillity, actions must be performed in their absoluteness, oneness and in totality, where there is sensitivity for all. This is where life takes us on a paradoxical ride where each one of us eventually has to decide either to use our mind as an instrument or be used by it under its cover of illusory fantasies.

Most of our lives are full of fantasies. We fantasize on everything: from the events of yesterday to those likely to take place tomorrow, forgetting the present moment. Existence only knows what exists in the present; it has no idea about the past or the future. It is our mind, which deludes us by separating the present moment into three fractions: the past, the present and the future. What is amazing is that the delusion of *who* we *were* is devastated when we decisively come to know the truth of *who* we *are* – simply nothing but aware conscious energy.

***

There are three levels of reality. When we comprehend the difference among these three, we are able to recognize the fantasies, the fallacies and the futility of the cognitive mind misleading and deceiving us by making us believe all that, which is not.

The first is existential reality. All that exists is as it is, the way it is, in 'the now' of every moment, while it lasts. Like a wave is factual and so is the ocean to which it belongs. It is an actual phenomenon for the duration that it lasts.

The second is our psychological reality. Here reality is illusory; it may seem or appear to be real, but may not be in its actuality. It is that observable reality of our cognition, which may also differ from one person to another. In other words, existence in this case is not the way we think it is. We may think of ourselves to be just body and treat the mind as a separate entity; scientifically, this is an optical illusion. We are all connected and made of quarks of energy, binding us together as an individual form. The fundamental reality is that all of us are the ultimate form of a unitary unified absolute energy in continuum.

For instance, the waves in an ocean rise and fall, but they do not exist independently; the ocean does. The wave has a momentary existence and is inseparable from the whole. Like in a gold ornament, the gold exists but the jewellery has no permanent existence of its own. In this manner, all that exists in our universe consumes and subsumes only one essential reality: the absolute energy.

The same holds good for individual consciousness,

momentarily existing separately like a wave, where the ocean here is the universal consciousness in the form of total awareness comprising the absolute spirit or energy. Individual conscious energy, though a part of the absolute awareness, gets attached to the dualities of existence, exhibited by the body and the mind in order to experience and realize life. All concepts of the physical self from our subconscious beliefs of ideas and images come and go like the waves in an ocean; what remains is the absolute awareness in the form of pure consciousness of who and what we are.

Both the soul and the individual self-conscious aware energy are distinct and intrinsic; one is the ocean and other the wave. The delusion arises when the mind, presuming its self-identity to be of me and mine, or body and mind, takes that to be factual, when the real us actually belongs to the absolute awareness, existing as the impersonal soul. This is where another spiritual concept arises that the form and the formless are one and not two. A wave is nothing but a part of that ocean; similarly we are nothing but a part of that absolute God or the soul residing within. We reveal our true identity or the real self only during our acts of selflessness with compassion for one and all. We then realize the oneness of the absolute signifying that we all are one.

***

The second level is also known as the 'relative reality', wherein the physical existence revolves as a continuous changing reality. It can be observed through our senses, which change according to time, person and space, relating everything in duality with opposites. For example, truths exist in relation to lies and love to hate. Each duality is interpreted by relating to its opposite.

For each one of us, existence is relative – happiness/sadness, good/bad, positive/negative, God/devil and so on. Nothing is good or bad, unless it is related to something meaningful for us. To physically exist with the cognitive mind, everything needs to be compared to or evaluated against its opposite. For example, to appreciate 'hot', we need to be aware of 'cold'. Something that is good for us may not be so for someone else. This again is relative and may not necessarily be true. Here lies the delusion. We are living in relative reality, which is constantly changing; if we are happy, we can be sure that sadness will soon follow.

***

The third level is known as the 'ultimate reality'. It is that reality, which is changeless, timeless, spaceless and eternal, indicating that all that exists is one and only aware energy within which transient interchangeable forms prevail. It does not support or contribute to any relativity, analysis or interpretation by the mind; it just exists as a unitary continuous absolute energy in continuum. It has no link to the past or the future, to emotions or to any planned evaluation, and to comparing or to judging. It does not connect to attachments or fears. It is reality in its total completeness in all respects. In the absolute sense, reality, truth, love or God are pure experiences of 'the now', which cannot be put into words. There is no duality here, and language being dual, words cannot relate them to the devil, lies or hatred.

The confusion arises between the realities of personal dual unconscious energy and those of the impersonal pure unitary consciousness, since they both simultaneously exist in the mind. Prima facie, both are inherent like a wave and an ocean or like a wave and a particle behaving in a subatomic structure; there has to be a transient existence for the process of the personal unconscious energy to first attach and relate itself to duality, experience life and henceforth evolve to transform into that impersonal consciousness. For this reason, the absolute raw energy first has to manifest itself in the form of absolute awareness in the mind and later extend to expand and evolve within the former awareness in making the mind conscious to experience and realize what life is all about.

Therefore, the presence of awareness requires physical existence to participate both as personal and also impersonal at the same time. Both God and the devil exist within our own mind, which, through our individual intensity of aware conscious energy, reveals and reflects the measure of delusions our mind is entrapped in.

***

Absolute energy applies the impersonal consciousness in making the mind aware of its own existential self to counter what the personal unconscious energy is experiencing in desire. This is how the journey of physical existence commences with delusions in considering the body and the mind to be the real self, until the impersonal consciousness, the divine within, awakens to enlighten the mind otherwise.

All concepts of mind, language and words come and go in the realms of dual and non-dual, since both are comprised of the same constituent, the absolute energy as one essential reality. Whether we consider this absolute as awareness, pure consciousness, wholeness, completeness, emptiness, nothingness and so on, we should never forget that what actually exists is only one and the rest are all but concepts of the mind trying to discover the ultimate truth of who and what we really are.

An attitude of giving along with silent acceptance of life's outcome is needed. We need to accept the present as it is and surrender our ego with grace and respect. In such self-awareness, both happiness and sadness, positive and negative, come closer towards their oneness: we do not get agitated or excited by either, as they are inseparable. We may control our actions through choices, but we cannot control the results. With the surrender of ego and in acceptance of reality, we will not react in fondness or aversion to any of our likes or dislikes.

Instead of clinging to our attachments or negating what we do not like, the mind-body interaction should observe, with spontaneous awareness any situation, more in the present moment with a proactive approach rather than react with a calculative mind brooding over events from the past into the future. If we follow such a practice, we will acquire the mental balance to face any reality, whether good or bad, with equanimity. Our existence in turn, shall lead us towards peace, fulfilment and completeness, away from the rollercoaster ride of choices and conflicts and likes and dislikes to a more relaxed path.

***

We can start by being more *observant* in the choices we make, which should be proactive rather than reactive. Then we should become *compassionate* and loving, not only towards our near and dear ones, but towards all around us. From here, we move on to the art of *giving*, rather than being concerned only about ourselves.

Truth comes next, i.e., being true to ourselves and making it a habit, even when we are pushed into a corner. We should have *faith*, because, without faith, life seems hollow, with constant doubts and suspicions pestering us, thus increasing conflicts and leading towards anxiety and suffering with sorrow.

***

Next comes the most difficult path to traverse, that of *non-attachment*, by surrendering the ego, the delusion within of 'I, me and mine', from everything. The root cause of our delusion stems from this emotional feeling of attachment to all that we think we have, whether in person or in kind, and the desire for accumulating more and more. It is imperative that when we make any effort, we should not be overly concerned or attached to its results.

***

Cause and effect, action and reaction or work and reward are all intrinsic to each other. We should definitely be concerned about the results of any of our efforts; anxiety and suffering enter only if and when we get attached to the results. So, it is attachment that we need to be careful about, which brings in fear, meaning we should not be attached to the fruits of its results. Attachments invite insecurity, bringing in the fear of incurring a heavy loss. *Fear* is the most negative emotion, having the power to destroy completely. So, lastly, we should control fear by drastically curbing the emotion to cling tenaciously to something. This is why it is said: Fearlessness is next to godliness.

***

Ancient Eastern philosophy proclaims that our existence is illusory, merely a play of the absolute spirit/energy in relativity or duality. All that we perceive simply superimposes itself on our consciousness and all that we believe, say, God and the devil, are simply concepts of the mind with no verifiable reality. What really exists is only the absolute, and we, along with all that exists, are a part of that. Knowing and experiencing the absolute is the only answer to disengage from the duality of positive and negative, cause and effect and so on. It is the only solution to counter fear and delusion, which our mind keeps creating by separating the absolute into the dual.

Spirituality believes only in oneness of the absolute where there is no duality to change or separate the life energy into one and many in forms of you and I. In the absolute, reality is changeless and blessed are those who can bring the dual back towards their centre, as near as possible, from where they separated. The methods applied in such a case are the mindfulness of being in the present and yoga for the unison among the body, the mind and the soul. We require a consciousness with astute awareness to help keep us away from delusions of duality played out by the mind, leading to rollercoaster rides marked by pleasure and pain as also success and failure.

Chapter 26

THE MEANING OF LIFE AND DEATH

If a man hasn't discovered something that he will die for, he isn't fit to live.

— Martin Luther King Junior*

The debate over the meaning of life and death dates back to the day when the first human walked this planet. For ordinary people, the concept of life and death is simply the time lived between birth and death. However, scientists, academicians, philosophers and religious scholars have different views about life and death.

Those who believe in science typically consider life and death as stages of our biological being, i.e., the physical existence of the human body. We may extend our life span a little more through multivitamins, herbal supplements, antioxidants, exercises, proper food and so on, but a day comes for certain when we die. Hence, life remains uncertain; but the one and only certainty it

---

*Martin Luther King Junior (15 January 1929 to 4 April 1968) was a respected American activist who played a leading role in the Civil Rights Movement (1954 to 1968).

provides is death. Our bodies are programmed for cell degeneration and there is nothing we can do about it. Death can strike any time; what we do not know are its exact time, place and form.

***

In the words of the pre-eminent William Shakespeare (1564 to 1616): 'Life's but a walking shadow, a poor player, that struts and frets his hour upon the stage, and then is heard no more; it is a tale told by an idiot, full of sound and fury, signifying nothing.' We should ask ourselves, after reading this snippet, if it is true or not.

What is the meaning of life? And what is its purpose? Is there life after death? What happens to our soul after death? Most of us get carried away by our emotions and sentiments and start believing to be true, without any concrete evidence, extraordinary incidents and stories floating around, especially on pastlife, regression, afterlife and so on. Very few people appreciate life, just as it is, without wondering too much about its meaning or its continuity after death.

***

We may refer to death as the end of our journey in life. We are so attached to our body and mind that no one wishes to die, not realizing that it is a beginning of a new life. However, those who have tasted life totally and are internally fulfilled embrace death. They have lived for today and for every day moment to moment.

Like any other form of energy, life too moves in a cyclic and circular manner. Every beginning comes to a certain point of end, but the same point also initiates another beginning for its next circular movement. Similarly, we notice the Earth moving around the Sun; from galaxies to seasons – all move in a circular pattern, which has no beginning or end. The same is the case with creation and destruction: in order to destroy, you first need to create and vice versa. All these factors indicate that life and death and creation and destruction are continuous and cyclical.

***

In life, there is only a beginning with no end. Energy has a tendency to expand and evolve; from a seed to a sapling to a tree to many more seeds, continuously repeating its cycle and forever expanding and evolving. The circumference of this circle keeps on increasing; life keeps on circling never meeting its end. Death is nothing but another beginning of life in its cycle of birth and death, constantly expanding and leading to more births.

***

Life is an opportunity. We may use it, misuse it, learn from its mistakes, evolve and move on with no regrets. However, the majority of us are worried, brooding over our past and anxious about the future, not knowing how to live in the present. We merely exist in illusions made up of a mixture of unconscious and conscious words, thoughts and deeds, not knowing what it is to be alive.

Life on its own has no meaning; it just exists. We can have any opinion; our personal experience of living could include interacting with others, socializing, deliberating on issues and consciously directing every situation. All such experience culminates in our reality. We affirm our stand on life and assert that we are responsible for, and have created, our own lives out of the existence provided to us. Therefore, we must focus more on living so as to understand the significance of life and bring some meaning to it.

Those who live in order to enjoy every single day as it comes are alert and aware of all that is happening around them. They wish to establish something in their life, earn their livelihood through honest means and feel worthy of whatever they do or are planning to do. For them, life is a challenge that needs to be undertaken, with positive ego and alert consciousness. They keep on observing things and experiencing life to become aware about themselves with the curiosity to know more about today, instead of brooding over the past and dreaming about tomorrow. Existence lived and experienced, moment to moment, consciously for today, is far more rewarding rather than having abundant knowledge and proving to others one's expertise in a variety of fields.

***

Here we are, holding on to life, not wanting death, and fearing to give up all those attachments and accumulations that we have clung on to for so long. It is only when we learn how to live truthfully and righteously that insecurity and fear disappear. We then learn the art of ageing, dying or disintegrating gracefully. We will consciously see death as a natural phenomenon of life. Fear and insecurity are like leeches, depleting our energy of life and bringing death faster and closer towards us.

We may pretend that we are not haunted by the thought of death. It is human nature to fear it to a certain degree. In many cases, the cause of the fear is more out of thinking of the physical pain, which we go through and the loneliness of old age, prior to death, rather than its actuality. Death strikes us in mysterious and unknown ways, especially when we are least bothered or when we are unaware of it. It is nearly impossible to predetermine death; life remains uncertain but never death. We simply have to face it, whether we like it or not.

Therefore, the cycle of birth and death continues endlessly. There are some, who observe and experience how the souls are behaving in this very life, while there are others narrating stories about how souls transmigrate into the next life. We can find a lot of material (printed or on the Internet) about life after death, reincarnation, transmigration of the soul, past life regression and so on. Here, I wish to present this subject not mystically but rationally, so that the reader can form an opinion with a free and open mind.

***

Like I have said earlier, life on its own does not have a meaning; living is a process, which creates a certain uniqueness reflecting our consciousness. It also has no purpose, because that would mean a goal, which again would restrict life only to materialism. How we reflect in totality should become the aspiration in the formation of our individuality, which remains in eternity after we die. This is how we remember the Buddha, Lord Krishna, Jesus Christ and many others for their uniqueness, which they left behind for eternity.

***

Spiritually, the mind needs to be aware and become conscious; where the present stage of past experiences is reflected by the consciousness of that being. It is also claimed that our soul or consciousness keeps moving after death to be reborn into another body, until it finally reaches its destination with purity in self-realization. In other words, the consciousness separated in duality, after realizing its true nature, merges back into its actual form of the absolute, as one.

In Hinduism and Buddhism, we have the prophecy of samsara and moksha. Samsara is that process of a continuous cycle of birth and death in its philosophy of reincarnation. It is related to the movement of the body and the mind in the form of karma, the cycle of action creating cause and effect. It relates to 'as you sow, so shall you reap', meaning the past creates the present, which, in turn creates the future.

Furthermore, samsara also elaborates that since we cannot easily comprehend the abstract idea of the infinite, eternal absolute and our intrinsic relationship to this non-dual Brahman, maya, through the mind, creates illusions separating us from the rest of reality encompassed in desires and attachments.

In order to grasp the ultimate reality, we are required to go through repeated cycles of birth and death until and unless our karmas comprehend and realize the oneness of all that exists without any separation whatsoever. Selfless karmas have the potential to liberate us from this web of samsara and realize moksha. It is that state in which both karma and samsara do not exist, representing the end of desire, attachment and its consequent suffering. This eventual state of oneness with the absolute reality is referred as 'self-realization'.

Therefore, the story of self-realization and what happens in the afterlife is again based entirely upon one's belief. In observable reality, we live in a material world of pleasure and pain, where the body and the mind exist in an illusory sense of separation, and we cling to that; here God and death become the most feared phenomena.

In order to comprehend the meaning of death, it is important that we first become aware of the illusions of existence. We will realize how everything in our life is so very transitory. Everybody comes and goes and so do we. We come from dust and go back into the same. There is no sense in grieving or clinging to any of our emotions or attachments. Wecome alone and empty-handed and shall return alone, carrying nothing. Life changes its bodily existence from one form to another, clearing the old to make way for the new. But we should always remember that those who leave a legacy behind never die.

***

The body may wither, the mind may cease working, we may doubt many things and life may remain uncertain, but what is definitely certain is death. It is always following us like a shadow and can strike at any time. It is an existential ongoing process, which is inevitable. Death is present in every moment: for instance, old cells dying and being replaced by new ones is not something of the future but happening at present constantly. We should live with the thought of death in the same way as we live with that of life, because they are intrinsic and inseparable from each other. We cannot conquer what we do not know; all that we can do is to live consciously and totally.

What is more important in life is living it rather than dying. We should look back and contemplate what contribution we have made in life to society and the world at large. Those who have lived their life totally do not fear death. Life is ordained for a purpose that is guided by something greater than we are. While some souls may be carefree, most of us experience the extremities of materialistic existence, which we sometime or the other wish to balance with spiritual grace. All we need to do is accept both the material and the spiritual with equal respect.

We often come across people who were once fully absorbed in their worldly life, stopping to ask: 'who am I?' Or 'what is the purpose of my life?' Ultimately, most of us realize the fact that the mind and the body are incomplete without the unison of the spirit. The spirit does exist and has its own significance. Spirituality can offer our body and mind the power to know the spirit, accept life with grace and realize that both are the same, i.e., the beginning and the end of any one span of physical existence.

***

The puzzling aspect is: who is God? Many seekers often ask this question to philosophers, spiritualists, scientists, pundits and padres. They provide a myriad of answers for this supernatural being who brings hope in our life. We may have our own beliefs and convictions regarding God, but it is not necessary that what we subscribe to is necessarily true. Spiritually, God has a form and is also formless. To put it differently: God is a part of us in the absolute spirit waiting to be experienced and realized by liberating ourselves from those samsaras of miseries and suffering, while we live in separation existing in duality. Spiritually, when the mind, the body and the spirit are fully realized as one in total awareness with pure consciousness, we are God realized.

When we think beyond rituals and beliefs, a spiritual yearning emerges from within. To a serious spiritual seeker, when materialistic renunciation takes place, a compassionate divine symphony is experienced, where all religions and everything seem one. A stage comes we experience our body and mind in selfless karma with compassion for that oneness in all. What we realize at that moment is nothing but God in such godliness. This occurs when the seeker (form) submerges deeply within the formless spiritual realm, realizing all that exists is only one and not two. Life and death subsume in themselves the completion of the final journey in totality as one.

Chapter 27

IN SEARCH OF OURSELVES

The best way to find yourself is to lose yourself in the service of others.

— Mahatma Gandhi

Finding one's self in the midst of those millions of thoughts that run through the mind is like finding the proverbial needle in a haystack. We are one, but our thoughts can function only through comparisons. As mentioned earlier, the mind requires two opposites to interpret what our senses perceive, whereas, when we refer to our self, there is only one.

The intellect separates the oneness into two in order to perceive anything. The mind relates to everything via thinking in terms of good/bad, positive/negative and so on, whereas the real self relates simply to that truth of who and what we are in totality as one and not separately. We are simply the state of our being. There exists a clear distinction between our mind and us. We can easily discover this distinction during those moments when we are witnessing or discovering our own mind playing games with us or with others.

***

When we prepare a resumé to describe who we are, the presentation normally reflects the personality of what the mind expresses. It is more of an objective summary of our outer persona relating to our physical and mental status in connection to the world that we exist in. However, when we observe the inner us, it is a different picture altogether. It becomes the subject of that state of our being, witnessing *who* we are and not the physical object of *what* we are. We will experience that we are different from our mind, since we can govern, alter and monitor our own mind. In fact, the mind is an instrument for us to use rather than be unconsciously used by it.

***

The state of our being represents the physical, mental, and spiritual aspects of our existence. We basically form a part of an interconnected and interdependent network of personal and professional aspects with regard to the environment surrounding us. When a problem surfaces in one aspect, it affects the other. Our emotions get unconsciously entangled, when we take our worries at the workplace home and vice versa. We constantly brood over the past, becoming anxious about our future. We live in a state of misery and suffering in spite of all the comforts and advancements that science and technology have provided us.

Science today is claiming that the state of our mind remains inordinately unconscious. Over 90 per cent of its functioning is derived from the subconscious and we seldom have control over it. Spirituality has been claiming the same for centuries. A human mind constantly lives in dreams of the past and the future impeding the present moment. The mind thrives on illusions of relativity and is simply not awake.

We exist in a world of dreams submerged in beliefs, bound with a conditioned and rigid 'me and mine', the cause of all our misery, anxiety and suffering. However, when we consider the state of our becoming a new entity by transforming ourselves, the emphasis shifts to the inner self; that innate spirit, which determines and controls the functioning of our mind and body. It encompasses the overall summation of our inner experiences, which the mind goes through while interacting with the relational world. It reflects more on that degree of our individual awareness, when the mind becomes conscious of what it perceives. The state of transforming with the aid of this inner self is that link between the universal creative intelligence in the form of aware energy connecting the human mind and body with all that it conceives. This affiliation of human experiences connects the universal awareness to the intellect of the mind. It, ultimately, determines and controls the mind resulting in what we have become in the form of our self-consciousness.

***

The whole objective of spirituality is to go beyond the duality of physical existence into that metaphysical presence of who we really are. The aforementioned resumé, which seeks to present our personality, does not disclose the real truth. Our inner self, comprising that unique individuality, is different from our outer personality. The mind presents only what others will appreciate in us, which may be true or not. However, when it comes to that inner self, the mind resists revealing it, arguing emotionally in self-interest (to reveal only what it desires to).

Our real self, after it attaches itself to the mind, goes on a rollercoaster ride in the domain of materialism and is trapped amidst various temptations, losing its real self and remaining ignorant of its true reality. The purity of our consciousness gets diluted due to lack of awareness. It reveals the supremacy of our unconscious mind over the spirit. This is a world of exclusiveness where we live in separation of me, mine and myself, personified with material attachments and not in that inclusiveness, which the universal spirit of oneness demands.

This in itself is a clear attestation of how mankind today is more concerned with the objectivity in materialism rather than the subjectivity of inclusiveness elaborated by spirituality. We have created exclusive religions, Gods, rituals, boundaries and governments to separate that inclusiveness, which is the rudimentary essence of our existence. The collective modern mind, from societies, institutions to religions, is simply supporting exclusiveness. In spite of acquiring tremendous resources in wealth, health and knowledge, anxiety and depression are still prevalent. Here is a clear indication that the unconscious mind running on auto mode is not aware of what it is doing, resulting in the chaos and turmoil, amidst which we all live.

***

From the foregoing discussion, the authenticity of my ideas and views should be apparent and also why we should become alert to focus our mind to treat this topic seriously. It is to make us aware that our real self has shrunk considerably and constricted itself to a minuscule percentage comprising our consciousness. This is the reason why we see today so much of double standards, deceit, swindling, violence, hatred and bloodshed all around. All this shows how little we know about our inner self, in spite of all that borrowed knowledge on spirituality that we rave about and proudly show off.

Those daily WhatsApp spiritual messages, which we receive while seeking inner peace and tranquillity, do not seem to make much of an effect. The cause originates from the unconscious mind, which is not aware of its true self. I repeat: neuroscientists have recently declared that over 90 per cent of our mind functions in an unconscious manner. This clearly indicates that our mind is running on its own track regulated by the power of the subconscious. In most cases, it does not question but blindly believes those thoughts, ideas and opinions, which have been planted by others. The cognitive mind does not provide us with that opportunity to know consciously 'who' and 'what' we really are. The intellect may question, but the spiritual witnessing mind simply makes us aware and conscious of all our unconscious acts, subject to our knowing of its existence. The cognitive mind, on the other hand, does not permit us to know the real self easily, being in a flux created by unconscious acts.

***

Spirituality seeks to free our mind from the past and the future. It also seeks to unite the body and the mind and lead them back to the determinant: the spiritual self. The secret is present only in one subject, which we call yoga, the path of unison for the mind, body and the spirit. Yoga is complete, only when its study and practice comprise all three entities. We seem to know a lot about our physical, mental and spiritual states, but how to unite them and transform their energies to observe, feel, experience and realize our ultimate self is the process given by yoga. It is that course of action, which is initiated by our will and effort. When the path is clear, awareness takes over and we sail through to easily reach our goal of unifying the mind, the body and the spirit. Everything that we see, feel and touch becomes inclusive, with nature and us merging into one.

***

The most important aspects of life – freedom, love, truth, reality and God – all seem to become ambiguous. Since they are purely experiential and beyond the cognitive mind, it unconsciously expresses them in fancy words and concepts. If we wish to comprehend these inner subtleties, we need to become aware and conscious to experience the same and not relate them through our subconscious to their polar opposites. If we do that, then the same differs from one person to another. The meaning and experience lie in their absoluteness and not by relating and separating them in dichotomies.

Freedom is that state when we can be truly ourselves. Our mind, burdened by numerous obligations, is bound to our family, friends, teachers, preachers, society, media and the government. It is further attached to traditions and rituals and is a victim of desires, wants, lust and greed. How can we be free with such a conditioned mind, which has no free space to create our own individuality?

We are a part of a herd called society and we are made to think in a collective, mundane manner, with rigid rules, terms and conditions. On top of all this, we have purveyors of organized religions telling us which God and guru to believe, how to tag along blindly, listen and act the way they want us to.

Our consciousness has become the slave of all those unconscious beliefs quietly working from the subconscious of our cognitive mind, reducing and limiting it to conditioned beliefs. This is how others try to control our life and why we almost always function unconsciously with regard to the past and the future. However, the present is ours; it cannot be taken over by anybody. It is as pure as it can be and the only hindrance coming between the presence of our present moment and the conscious self is the mind carrying a heavy baggage of the past and the future.

***

We should silence the mind and allow serenity to set in. We then enter the realm of our personal experiential self where freedom, justice, love, compassion and truth are prevalent in 'the now'. When the thinking mind withdraws, our spirit comes to the fore. There comes a choiceless awareness to observe the present moment, alert with attention, without allowing the mind to think, choose and analyse in self-interest. This is the reason I emphasize that freedom today is more about being a rebel from all prior conditioning. We can never be at peace with a conditioned mind. So, we have three choices – rebel against all beliefs and dictates, renounce them or reflect carefully on who and what we are and how we would like to change ourselves.

***

If we choose the third option, meditation is very beneficial. Meditation leads to emptying the mind of all the unwanted stuff accumulated there. Silence is that expanse from which one awakens and the chattering of the mind is that encumbrance within which one remains in an unconscious dream. We need to create such a meditative space, where we individually determine the mind's course of action. The mind should experience everything on its own without any past beliefs or fear of the future by not attaching itself to any emotional desires. Only then, shall there be creativity, purpose and truth in our existence, which we may consider as self-experienced and realized under free will by us, from and for ourselves.

***

Celebrities in all fields will keep on talking about ensuring peace and justice or provide us with this or that suggestion for an ideal state of affairs. If we look at the world around us, we can easily gauge how much peace *really* exists. Invariably, we find only anxiety and despair in almost all parts of the globe. What is the solution to the numerous problems faced by humankind? No outside source can provide us that freedom which we deserve. Only when we learn the art of being, knowing and becoming experientially, shall we attain wisdom in self-experience and understand what life is all about. When our self awakens, we shall experience and realize a life far beyond the confines of wealth, material accumulations, attachments and desires.

***

It is very easy to claim that we know ourselves. Normally, we do so only from our cognitive senses and, that too, objectively. The subject of our inner selves within remains a mystery. Transformation starts the day we realize we are beyond our cognitive mind, because the moment we utter 'our mind' or 'our brain says this' and so on, we realize that our real self is not the mind but it is merely our instrument. We are simply and unconsciously confined to what our mind dictates. When we gradually get rid of this ignorance, we begin to observe and discover things: how our mind keeps chattering about the past and the future situations, using us like a puppet. This is the part and the path, which we need to consciously observe in silence with the power of our insight.

We are suspended between matter and the spirit: the outer persona that we exhibit so arrogantly and also the core inner serene individuality. Unless we are aware of both, we shall remain incomplete and disturbed. I repeat: the mind in its material world is always bubbling in action relating one factor to another, in order to choose and indulge in for its desires in self-interest. In this process, the mind unconsciously limits itself only to what it believes from past knowledge and conditioning.

We can imagine how an unconscious mind, without a navigator, can become detrimental in a collective society. Such an individual simply lives in a society, but remains alone in self-centredness, functioning only for his ego. He gets lost mindlessly in 'me, mine and myself', not realizing that there is much more to life than only material possessions and carnal desires.

***

What we see today is that there is no freedom of individual consciousness, thought or action and hardly any scope left to create or build up our own individuality. Eventually, we become a part of that herd, referred to as community, in which we eat, drink, sleep and reproduce. An uncontrolled mind in such cases has no option but to function on auto-mode unconsciously. It is only when we become aware of any situation that the mind becomes conscious and alert to focus without being diverted here and there. There are always a few who stand out against these norms laid down by others and create their own legacy. Whether in the material world or the spiritual one, they excel in whatever they attempt with their own intuitiveness, intention and integrity.

Freedom emerges the moment we rebel from rigid conditioning and start thinking in our personal capacity as individuals. Most of us are not under any pressure, except occasionally, and can think freely. We become aware and conscious of what we do and also become responsible for repercussions that follow. We do not provide any explanations and do not give excuses for our actions; also, we do not blame others for our wrongdoing. For that matter, we even do not attribute everything to destiny.

We become agnostics and skeptics to the outside world because we do not believe blindly what others tell us. We do not feel the need to pray to an outside God, go to temples or churches or other religious places and follow their rituals and dogmas. We surrender our mind to accept inwardly that God resides within, in our acts of selflessness with compassion for all as one. There is a certain quietness and free space in our mind, which is not overloaded with the conditions set down by others.

Our spirit is now free to 'breathe' with its own uniqueness to determine and control the subconscious mind by not allowing it to wander here and there. A limited mind is restricted and driverless, running unconsciously on others' wishes and desires. Meditation provides us with the methods on how to empty our conditioned and rigid mind. It makes us dynamic and mindful, eliminating the past and future thoughts to enter the present. This present moment is that silent period, when our spirit is free from past and future conditioning, without any limitations on the mind to create, experience and realize what it really wishes.

There is no need for us to seek peace or happiness from the outside world dictated by others. Everything lies within for us to experience with our own inner awareness. There is no need for a separate personal God to be provided to us again by others under rigid conditions. God simply resides within, wanting us to 'experience' Him with our acts of absolute selflessness. So long as we are attached to our desires, we will remain alone and separate and shall never be able to experience that real self, continuing to suffer due to conflicts between one choice and another. Our real self does not exist with a separate mind and body. It prevails in the presence of that aware energy, which is a part of a unitary, unified consciousness existing in the form of absolute aware energy.

***

To consider physical existence as illusory or unreal is a falsification. It is more out of ignorance, since it is only out of this existence, that the body and mind can discover the Divine. The absolute energy always remains changeless, timeless and spaceless, but within this infinite zone, it expresses itself in many interchangeable forms that constantly evolve so that we can experience what matter and spirit are all about. What we need to remember is that any object – in our case being the body and mind – always remains a part of its subject. Therefore, if the whole is real, so are its parts; the object is also real. Matter and spirit may represent dichotomies in order to discern, discriminate and choose between this and that, but ultimately they are a part of the same subject. Therefore, our mind may wander here or there; however, our spirit requires that abode within, to experience and realize how to create its own unique self.

Chapter 28

THE CONCEPT OF COMPLETENESS

That is complete this is complete. From that completeness comes this completeness; if completeness is taken away from completeness, only completeness remains.

— Isha Upanishad

The above verse from one of the ancient scriptures of India defines the completeness of the absolute as well as that of the relative; even after we separate one from another, only completeness remains. Normally, if we take something out of something, the quantum of content of the first entity is bound to reduce. However, the Upanishads disagree with this contention. The Upanishads claim that if we take something away from the infinite nothing is reduced, since we cannot take out anything from the infinite. However, the world is finite with a limited quantity of everything. If we take away something from this world, elementary mathematics should apply and the matter in the source should reduce. So, let us see how we can interpret this completeness based on the epigraph to this chapter.

***

The doctrine underlying the Advaita* Upanishad asserts all that exists is not two. Every entity is complete in all respects and maintains its basic character: that of being the absolute in every aspect. In the manner a seed is complete, so is a sapling, a flower, a tree, fruits and many more seeds that the fruit will bear in future. All are complete in their own respective manner, just like the whole cycle of life requires its finishing in totality for its wholeness.

This doctrine further explains how, in the universe, even though infinite but within which, through the concepts of matter, time, space, cause and effect, the mind reveals the transient nature of the finite. In both cases, the basic ingredient of the universe remains the same as absolute spirit/energy, complete and constant, whether it is present in the finite or the infinite. It only changes its expression for a short while displaying its properties in different forms.

***

The approach of the Upanishads is to elaborate on the wholeness of life: how to live in totality. We should lead a wholesome life full of possessions and comforts in materialism and but also be able to transcend towards that spirit, by not attaching ourselves to either. Every human being comprises both the matter in body-mind and the abstract in the form of aware consciousness. The former thrives in relativity and the latter in the absolute. We have to live in both and not to choose between them. The former is meant for materialism and the latter for spiritualism. It is only after living in the former that we may transcend to the latter.

*Advaita literally means 'not two'.

The phenomenon of finiteness exists, irrespective of the finite continuously altering its form of expression from its fundamental absolute character. Whether in totality or by its innate separation into its relative finite attribute, the intrinsic absolute, however, always remains constant and complete in all respects. This philosophy has been a great source of inspiration in the formation of quantum thermodynamics, related to two independent scientific theories: thermodynamics and quantum mechanics.

In a similar manner, science explains that energy is infinite and its fundamental structure remains constant and complete in the form of the absolute. However, within this framework, it changes by expressing itself in various interchangeable transitory forms, becoming finite and also relative in forms of solids, gases and liquids. The fundamental source remains the same as the basic absolute energy, but during its field of operation, like in the case of electricity, the same energy separates relatively into positive and negative. The sky remains the same as the absolute, not affected by time, space and causation, but what it reflects during the day and the night is relative and prone to change. Science reveals that every facet of relativity, even though complete in its own aspect, has the absolute truth of singularity at its centre.

***

In humans, the absolute energy manifests itself in two primary facets: first, matter as the finite, consistently changing in its forms, and the other manifesting as abstract spirit, the unchanging entity in the mind. On its own, the absolute is dormant, representing nothing, but dark energy. However, in the form of matter, it represents the objective observable reality, becoming the domain of science in the latter, as awareness, which remains the subjective reality becoming more of a study in spiritualism.

From that nothing in the infinite universe emerges the something called aware conscious energy or spirit, which becomes everything in the form of consciousness to oversee and reflect life during its transient period in a specified finite space and time. Therefore, since we consist both of matter and consciousness, both need to conjoin in their wholeness. We cannot choose one over another, irrespective of whether one is illusory and the other is not. The ultimate ingredient of both remains the same as the absolute. They are simply one appearing as two emerging out of the same reality.

The Upanishads say: do not create a separation. We should enjoy the outer world with inner awareness. It is only the mind, which separates everything into its duality making us unconscious. We should also listen to that witness, who is the actual us and not the mind. The inner us is conscious of what the mind does but in no way a part of our cognitive thoughts. The moment we experience and realize this inner us, we will be in totality with the outer, and the absolute witness will become one with the relative mind.

This is what life in the absolute and its relative existence in physicality are all about. We should not negate anything; we should be aware and just go 'beyond' to live in the moment. We should also go above and transcend ourselves, watch our own thoughts, feelings and action in all that we do. In other words, we should not get attached or identify ourselves with either the material or the spiritual. Both are parts of that same completeness; they just require their respective finishing to rejoin in their totality as one. By separating any energy, the mind goes away from the centre of its oneness to the outer edge of its circle of operation.

***

Matter displays innumerable properties of interchangeable forms and formless features like structure, motion, space, time and information, displaying different parts of universal forms as the observable reality. These are basically objects and processes, which the mind manifests and perceives from the totality of the universe. Not only that, even thoughts and emotions are objective forms, existing within the duration of space and time. In the relative world, the absolute continuously changes, expands and evolves, reflecting the respective properties of that object. Therefore, in spirituality, anything in which changes occur within space and time becomes the study of the objective realm. That which remains infinite, constant and changeless represents the subjective world of the unchanging aspects.

The nature of reality comprises both the absolute and relative, i.e., matter and the consciousness. In other words, the world of dualism in the form of matter and that of the spirit in the form of awareness are subsumed into the completeness of its totality representing the subject as One. It reveals the presence of the ultimate, supreme absolute reality of awareness, which has the ability to make the mind aware and conscious to decode the same and be able to perceive all that the universe offers. It was referred to during those ancient days as the 'Para-Brahman' (the highest Brahman). The mind is entitled to give any name to this supreme reality such as Creator, God or Atman.

I repeat: the absolute has the ability to express itself in many interchangeable forms, on its own, however, remaining the same. Out of all its attributes, the absolute has only one single attribute for its own self, which is the power of awareness for its own energy to comprehend all other forms of energies already referred to as Para-Brahman.

The universe is that passive state of Brahman, the omnipotent absoluteness in which all diverse concepts like reality, soul, God, consciousness and matter in unity as well as in diversity exist. Therefore, energy, the name given by science, is complete as one, whether it reflects in the absolute or refracts in its relative character. There are three laws of thermodynamics in science, which are assigned to this phenomenon.

The first law of conservation of energy states that the total energy of an isolated system is indivisible and remains constant; energy can be transformed from one form to another, but cannot be created or destroyed.

The second law states that the state of any field of energy increases in entropy when dispersed from its source into the infinite, thereby bringing down its quality.

The third law asserts that this entropy reaches its passive state at the level of shunya or zero, when the thermal aspect reaches its lowest.

All these laws are well inscribed in the Upanishads. The first is in the form of the absolute energy's totality or completeness remaining constant in every aspect, as described in the Shanti (peace) Mantra (given in the epigraph to this chapter). The second explains how the field of energy, Shakti, disintegrates into entropy losing its quality when it goes further away from the source of its force, i.e., Shiva. In the manner, when light energy emitted from the Sun disperses into the infinite universe, it loses its quality never to return to its source or force of energy. And third, that state of zero or shunya, the ultimate passive state of the absolute explaining the nothingness in the universe in totality. It is symbolized as the source of cosmic power called Shiva, which is revealed in one of the holiest Hindu shrines believed to be over five thousand years old at the Amarnath cave high in the Himalayas in Jammu and Kashmir. Shiva as the absolute is manifested there in the form of the Jyotirlingam* existing at subzero temperatures in the form of a stalagmite.

Lord Shiva is considered to be the liberator as well as the destroyer. Whatever begins has to end by coming back eventually to its own point of beginning in order to restart another cycle, even if it takes billions of years. From the microcosm to the macrocosm, all follow this cyclical pattern of the universe, irrespective of time and space and whether science in its objective study agrees to such a theory or not.

I repeat: energy is both absolute and relative, but, in its basic substance, the absoluteness remains as the one and only essential reality. However, while operating actively within its own field, energy continuously changes from one form into another, randomly, in entropy. It also becomes illusory when relating itself to its polar opposite. This is because it is only in the absence of one that the relative or the other factor is revealed. In the absence of heat, it becomes cold; in the absence of light it becomes dark; and in the absence of godliness, we experience the devil within.

In reality, they are all one and not two. It is only a case of separation of the absolute into its diversity and not in its division. All opposites are intrinsic and inherent to each other as one, being two sides of the same coin. The

---

*The Jyotirlingam represents Lord Shiva. Jyoti means 'radiance' and lingam (phallus) is the symbol of Shiva.

source remains the absolute, but on separation from its oneness in duality, it gets related to its opposite forming two ends of the same whole.

***

Therefore, it becomes very difficult for the mind to define or describe the absolute truth. If we really wish to describe it, we have to simply declare truth as that which exists as it is in its absolute real form. It cannot be defined with words, thoughts or feelings; it is not a concept for it identifies with only, what is, as it is. The abstract element of truth is so vast that the whole universe gets included in it. However, we also know that the absolute, in order to experience physical existence, separates into its duality relating itself to its opposite. Relative truth in this category, though temporarily real, exists with its opposite in the form of a lie, but within the limitations of time, space, cause and effect.

Absolute truth is that reality, which exists permanently as it is, without being affected by any limitations. In relative truth, there is something connecting to something else. The absolute truth is boundless, timeless, nameless and changeless and is not dependent on any God or the devil. Its properties only change, differentiating one from another during the transient period marked by limited space and time.

Every relative aspect, which the mind perceives and relates to in order to conceptualize for its comprehension gets separated into its duality. It becomes the object of that subject, whether it is truth, reality, God or love. Between any subject and its objective part, there is a certain relationship; we are either on one extreme or another. Like in the case of the witnessing self, it is that presence of *who* we are, that intensity or degree of individual awareness, the subject of life. It witnesses the object, the mind or ego and a body-mind-soul relationship is created.

However, aware energy is that Para-Brahman, the core from which the act of witnessing takes place. This centre represents the totality of that oneness: the absolute truth or reality where there is no subject/object relationship, all that exists is one. The further we go away from our centre, the higher will be the quantum of pain and suffering.

***

As explained above, the absolute is essentially nameless and without attributes, i.e., boundless in nothingness. In the omnipotent absolute, concepts of reality, soul, God, matter and consciousness exist in unity as well as in diversity. In this infinite space, the individual consciousness, after being aware, becomes active in order to experience life and, ultimately, returns to its passive state of Brahman. Therefore, at times, it becomes difficult for a rational mind to digest that the active soul, returning on death to its absolute dormant nothingness, transmigrates intact through this unified field of consciousness and again enters another body and mind.

***

As noted earlier, in actuality, all the three, the body, the mind and the soul, remain as one absolute intrinsic structure and represent themselves, respectively, as gross, subtle and core energies. In every fresh cycle of birth and death, each one appears in a fresh body and mind with a certain degree of awareness to create a new soul. A lot also depends upon the individual's genetic framework, which through the reproductive cycle acquires some remnants from the past.

I repeat: from one lifetime to another, every human being is a fresh amalgamation of body, mind and soul representing the absolute through its witnessing aware energy and the relative through cognition. In ignorance, the intellectual perception reflects only the relative aspect. However, if spiritually awakened, the intuitive perception reveals the completeness of both as one eternal absolute reality. There are many other interpretations to this theory; all of us are entitled to our own opinions and beliefs.

***

It is only in totality of its completeness in the nature of its actual absolute reality that we are able to comprehend the infinite awareness by which the universe exists and we exist. We presume a lot in ignorance, believing the unfinished relative reality, though complete in its own respect, however still remaining a separated part of that absolute as our sole personality, due to which we suffer. Hence, it is imperative for us to understand the infinite nature and experience and realize our energies in totality to wrap up all accomplishments in totality within the completeness of our existence.

Only we, as the absolute self, have the mind that can transform the energy from the cosmos into aware conscious energy. In such a state of finished completeness, we shall find the wholeness in totality of the absolute reality of truth, love, 'the now', God and so on.

To simplify further, the mind, having its own reasons to experience life, separates the absolute energy into two, living in a paradox thinking one is better than another. It does not realize they incorporate two sides of the same constituent in their respective oneness. This separation is the cause and effect of one's misery and suffering, which spirituality attempts to point out that bliss is attainable only when these two polar opposites merge back totally in their centre of oneness. Normally, during physical existence, realizing this state of equilibrium or absoluteness is more of a vision; we simply need to strive for that, in order to come as near to our centre as far as possible. Every activity is understood by the mind only after we compare one object or activity, relating that separately to its antithesis; what we forget here is that the synthesis of both exists only in their centre. Therefore, absolute realization and maintaining this equilibrium, that too in passiveness, is more of inspiration.

As mentioned earlier, God and the devil both are within us, one as the witnessing self and the other as ego. It is more through experiencing rather than knowing that will take us towards the centre of our being. We will keep on living in duality, swinging from one end to another. All that one is required to do is to balance the material with the spiritual and be consistently aware at all times.

Spiritual empowerment or enlightenment is an overpowering and overwhelming mystery. A guru or teacher should only point towards that direction for us to experience and realize life in our own personal manner. We can also gain knowledge from any authentic source including books. As spiritual seekers, we will learn and understand many concepts; even if they differ, they will all lead us only towards one destination: Oneness. It is only after we discover our true self, the mind reveals the degree of our conditioning: whether we are existing in blind beliefs or following others' experiences, rigid in our own way of thinking or are we free to know and experience everything on our own.

Chapter 29

AWARENESS IS EVERYTHING

Aware energy, on its own is nothing; existing in spaceless, timeless, limitless dark energy. However, on manifesting itself within the mind, it becomes everything: where awareness is the presence and that presence is the awareness. Like zero is nothing, manifesting itself with other integers, it becomes everything.

— Gian Kumar

Everything, meaning all that we see, feel and touch that the mind thinks and creates, and every single activity of our existence are but reflections of our consciousness from the underlying presence of an entity called awareness. It is the one and only presence, which makes our mind conscious to experience the universe in various different forms. Even while we are reading or performing some other activity, it is our awareness that is making it possible. It is only because we are aware that we exist that life has any meaning; otherwise existence itself would have no meaning. Our mind has the ability to become aware of both: its own awareness and also of what it perceives.

***

Energy can be in various forms: absolute to relative, psychic to nuclear and so on. When raw energy enters the mind, it manifests itself as awareness and triggers the mind into action. It is that quality of being awake at any present moment. Awareness stirs up the mind and makes it alive, allowing thoughts to emerge. Awareness comes prior to every other function of the mind.

It is the presence and the intensity of this aware energy, which witness all that the mind does. It is that presence, which does not require either any seer or what is being seen; it is pure seeing in 'the now'. It is changeless awareness watching the flow of energy, which is being transmitted here and there, and retaining its absolute nature in totality.

***

Our bodies are different from one to another; it is the mind functioning under the extent of space and time that separates the psychic energy into dual opposites to choose and discern. However, the aware energy remains intact and absolute witnessing the mind in all that it does. Awareness alone exists in perpetuity and, within its ambit, we have a continuous transformation from form to formless, expanding and evolving for life to experience what existence in duality is all about.

***

Awareness begins from awareness and returns to it and nothing besides awareness exists for very long. From nothing comes that something, which is everything to us and goes back into that nothing. We as body and mind disappear; what remains finally is only that aware energy existing in the electromagnetic field of the universe constantly responding, reflecting and refracting from one source to another.

The mind basically is nothing but a process of movement of one thought meeting another. It is the brain that exists, not the mind. The mind sustains itself by mechanically chattering in the absence of our presence. However, when we watch and witness in silence, looking intensely into the mind, thoughts disappear and the actual us as that presence of awareness emerges. If and when we observe inwardly in silence and watch our own thoughts, we will become aware of the distance that we have created between our perceptive thoughts and ourselves as awareness. Accordingly, we create a separate identity in our mind.

In the first stage, what we have is only the presence of the 'being' in silent watchfulness, which is without any choice or judgement. From this source of pure, fresh and aware energy, we get the first apprehension of any present moment. Meaning, at this particular moment, that is during the initial process of imbibing, aware energy covers both the observer observing that moment and the object being observed are one. Thoughts, which arise during this moment, are also choiceless and without any discrimination.

In this stage, I repeat, the observer, through observing (mind) grasps the object being observed, and the mind is still at this moment. It is later when the mind becomes attentive that this awareness expands by activating the mind to become conscious and think. Thoughts emerge and separate this aware energy into its relative duality and the process of expansion and evolving is initiated for us to become something in life.

Therefore, gradually within this absolute awareness behaving as the watcher or the witnessing self, thoughts move and express themselves. Thoughts connected to the outside get attached to the inner desires in the mind. The mind then becomes alive in consciousness and realizes its real form. In other words, from within the infinite comes the finite; from the changeless, the mind moves towards change; and from the formless awareness is reflected in the perception of form. Ideas, images and concepts appear and arise in the form of thoughts in the mind.

***

The second stage begins after the mind separates absolute energy into duality, relating everything to its opposites in order to think and choose so as to become conscious and experience the desires of life. One thought after another enters the mind. Thinking means movement, pursuing ideas, beliefs and opinions, adding knowledge with experience and so on. Existence prevails primarily through movement by thinking, choosing, indulging and experiencing, relating through the quality of our thoughts to what we desire. It progresses to that stage of becoming the form of our consciousness from its initial state of being.

***

The third stage now commences: after awareness has settled in the mind and thoughts have comprehended the relativities of existence, they get stored in the subconscious or the memory/data bank of the mind. This storehouse, in turn, forms our behavioural patterns, resulting in the formation of our habits in likes and dislikes. After that, the mind goes on a running mode of its own maintaining all its functions in an unconscious manner, deriving data from the subconscious, without requiring any further consciousness or awareness out of that past conditioning.

However, there still remains a small percentage of our conscious mind, which is responsible for intensifying the mind to acquire and supplement further awareness to master and tame the unconscious part of the mind.

Awareness is that crucial element, which transforms our old habits into new.

***

Ridiculous as it may seem, it is extremely hard for any mind to comprehend the idea of an abstract, impersonal spirit to be representing, as its own presence, the spirit of awareness. Moreover, the mind is designed mechanically to be aware of whatever it perceives through its five senses. However, when it comes to recognizing it own self, it is simply not aware of its own presence, which it has the full capacity to do so. Meaning, it is not aware in what direction the thoughts, emotions and actions are flowing.

The mind as well as the consciousness has been so conditioned over centuries – vis-à-vis what society demands from ancient traditions, cultures, communities, name, family and gender to all religious identities – that it becomes fully subsumed in one's ego consciousness.

Therefore, unless the mind frees itself from its past and future conditioning, whatever efforts an individual makes towards spirituality go in vain because of such limitations.

We do not seem to realize is that energy in whatever form is constantly aware. From a subatomic particle to the electromagnetic field of the universe, there is a constant interaction. Each form of energy responds, reflects, refracts, absorbs and assimilates to convert from one form into another. It is only the human mind, which has this additional ability to diffuse its aware energy by enhancing that into a conscious field, which, unfortunately, one is not aware of.

It is for the aforementioned reasons that there is a tremendous gap between the presence of 'who we are' and 'what we have become' and neuroscientists can comfortably claim that the mind is fundamentally an unconscious mechanism of the brain.

Since the mind is primarily designed to function in duality in an unconscious momentum, it constantly swings from one extreme to another. It has been conditioned to think of itself only as body and mind forgetting the third element, the spirit as the presence of awareness, which has the ability to master the mind from its unconscious operations.

Hence, the mind does not easily accept this fundamental fact that essentially it is nothing but awareness. The mind relishes its own material existence in ego consciousness with its thoughts of 'me, mine and myself' as supreme. The mind in such a manner remains unconscious unless one becomes aware and conscious of the ego in order to master and regulate, when it gets attached to material possessions and carnal desires purely in self-interest.

Therefore, awareness is that subject of 'who' we are and the quantum of what we perceive and experience becomes the object or the content of 'what' we are in the form of our consciousness. Awareness reflects the state of our mind; consciousness in return reflects the state of our awareness. Consciousness is the sum total of what we are representing: the degree or the quality of our awareness. Both combine to master the mind, which, if ignorant, not only runs in its own unconscious mode but also takes charge by dictating to us its own 'terms and conditions'.

***

If we remain still and silent, being alert and observing our own thoughts, we will realize that we are not the mind but the spirit in awareness. The moment we become conscious, we will notice one thought after another come and go; also perceptions and sensations come and go. It is awareness, which is effortlessly watching all this. We are nothing but that space of awareness, which reveals in silence all that the mind thinks and perceives. We are that awareness covered in sheaths of subtle energy in an unconscious state called the mind enfolded with further layers of gross energy called the body.

Thoughts develop from ideas and images change into concepts, going from the present into the past and projecting that into the future. However, as long as we are immersed in awareness, watching everything silently, we are in the presence of our being. Awareness, therefore, is that state of mind, which determines our aliveness. In other words, the actual existence of our body and mind is proportionate to the level of its awareness.

The state of awareness in any human being remains partial and incomplete, because the mind is unconsciously doing its job of separating the oneness of aware energy into its duality in relativity. The mind is constantly thinking, reasoning, judging and choosing to indulge in, experience and realize this or that, purely in self-interest for its self-preservation. Consciousness is required throughout this psychic process to determine its consequences, because it is responsible for becoming what we are. If awareness is the state of the mind, then consciousness represents the quality of that mind. Both awareness and consciousness in their functioning are close to each other and likewise reflect upon one another; without one, the other cannot exist.

***

Let us now probe this area of mind rationally and cautiously, but not in the manner that religion demands. Both awareness and consciousness are highly significant for spiritual empowerment, because the subject of spiritualism primarily revolves around these two words. Very few individuals have attempted to elaborate on spiritualism by differentiating between awareness and consciousness.

As noted earlier, physical existence, as we know is a state of kinetic energy. The fundamental ingredient is the absolute energy, which can neither be created nor destroyed, and in its fundamental state remains static, potential, constant, meaning indivisible and changeless. However, when this dormant energy is assimilated by the mind, it manifests itself as awareness, while retaining its absolute identity.

Therefore, within this changeless state, changes occur. The mind first becomes aware in order to later become conscious and experience life by forming its own level of consciousness. Life gives a shape to its existence, where the relevance shifts more from its state of being (awareness) into the state of becoming (consciousness).

At one end, we have the state of mind as awareness and, at the other; we have the quality of mind in the form of consciousness. Both function simultaneously in unison for the mind to discover what it really wishes and desires. The total quotient, I repeat, barely totals up to 5 per cent in the functioning of the mind. The rest of the mind's functioning is done unconsciously in auto mode, leading to unbridled thinking and even to the desire to unleash mayhem and violence. This is the reason why there is so much of unrest, turmoil and bloodshed in this world of ours. Meditation in mindfulness is one of the practices provided by spirituality to enhance the aware mind to become more conscious and take charge of what the mind does and should do.

Awareness comes first and consciousness follows, both to expand and evolve: one as the force and the other as its field. The former is the immortal cosmic God, Shiva, within which the latter, his consort Shakti, is the field of consciousness. The former is the core and the latter its subtle form; both are a part of one another, with both wishing to come nearer to each other for attaining that completeness in totality. Achieving that state of equilibrium, where all the three – body, mind and spirit – wish to become one, is referred to as self-realization.

This state, during our lifetime can never be realized, because equilibrium can never be sustained in separation during dual existence in relativity. In reality, the field of consciousness, because of incessant random thoughts, goes into entropy. The moment it distances itself from its source of awareness, its quality suffers and, gradually, it disintegrates losing its own capability. Eventually, it returns to its state of nothingness in infinity. This has been well explained by the second law of thermodynamics and also by the awesome tandav nritya (cosmic dance) of Nataraja, another name for Lord Shiva, meaning 'the king of dance'. As per Hinduism, for this reason, Shiva, besides being the liberator, has also been ordained as the destroyer. If equilibrium cannot be retained or sustained, only various transient forms, which are bound to change, disintegrate and return to their changeless state of the absolute.

***

Therefore, in awareness, there is no doing or becoming. It is the job of the consciousness, which transforms itself, trying to seek its completeness with totality in self-realization. It does not realize the futility that what it is seeking is nothing other than that which can be found in itself. Therefore, the core that is awareness remains as the force behind this psychic energy and consciousness constantly tries to manage its centrifugal property within its field.

Technology keeps expanding in our material world by leaps and bounds at a much faster pace than human consciousness. The wants keep increasing and technology continues to supply, but the quality of our inner consciousness is devalued due to attachment to incessant desires. Each one of us is clinging to 'me, mine and myself', which happens mainly because of the growing distance between one human being and another due to self-interest.

Such degradation of our consciousness with progressive destruction in our values will ultimately diminish, demean and disperse it (consciousness) into oblivion, which is bound to happen one day, even if it takes millennia. It is entirely up to our awareness as to how and when we become conscious of this inevitable disaster and devise better and more effective methods to postpone this catastrophe from happening.

***

We are plundering this earth for our self-interest to such an extent that, despite spectacular advances in science and technology, we will soon no longer be able to sustain the biological ecosystem. Due to mental degradation in a predominantly industrial civilization marked by strife and lust for power, we notice a gradual shift in our human values. We are going away from compassion in life towards a destructive culture with a feeling of indifference to all that is happening around us.

We humans need to wake up and become aware of the reality that technology and materialism alone cannot help us survive. It is imperative that we understand the basic definition and the meaning of life, spirit and spiritualism and practise the same sincerely. It makes no sense to lecture others intellectually on high moral values and ranting artificially on such values. We need to correctly balance our material wealth with spiritual wisdom in order to attain comfort for the body, peace for the mind and joy for the spirit.

***

For the sustenance of joy and peace, what we require is to be more pragmatic in our study of spiritualism, instead of merely repeating our ancient scriptures, which were meant for particular periods in history. Today, we need to self-inquire, self-examine and self-discover that truth with regard to love, compassion, God and the nature of our own reality.

We need to be alert, attentive and authentic in order to be able to comprehend this choiceless awareness before the mind and its intellect separate the same into two. For this to happen, the methods of mantra, meditation and mindfulness are considered necessary in making the mind focused, still and quiet to enhance the intensity of our awareness. Creativity and intuitiveness are strong examples of choiceless awareness, which has brought forth every single invention in this materialistic world of ours.

Our level of awareness is always in the present and not in the cognitive mind operating in the past or the future. In the present moment, we can be creative, watchful and alert, thereby surrendering to its reality. The present does not give us time to think, whereas, for thinking, time is of the essence. That is why, on the one hand, thoughts mainly relate to the outside world, where we plan our future from experiences of the past. On the other hand, meditation is advised for the inner world and the inner self. Thoughts can never be spiritual; they are always submerged in desire for something or the other. When we are experiencing anything in the present, it is awareness more in the knowing and not in the thinking. This dimension of psychic activity is considered to be spiritual.

Thinking reduces us to our ego consciousness, identifying with the body and the mind, known mainly for material attachments and carnal pleasures, besides the latter being a victim of rigid beliefs. Through the mind, thinking could create an *impression* that we are spiritual. The doctrine of spirituality simply follows the principal of oneness, in total awareness with pure consciousness, which can only be experienced in the present moment with the minimum of thoughts.

***

Self-help is currently a serious subject of study in this chaotic world of ours. For those who feel incomplete in life, spirituality seems to have a direct connection with self-help. In fact, spirituality has a strong link because a psychiatrist may try to repair the mind with medicines and other techniques or a psychologist may attempt to alter the mind's thinking processes. However, spirituality will basically upgrade and transform a mind and elevate it towards a higher consciousness aiming for totality, material as well as spiritual, in order to bring that oneness in our life.

When the mind is disturbed, psychic means of self-help will provide us with anti-depressants to treat our anxiety and suffering. These treatments are bound to have a number of unpleasant physical side effects like nausea, deficient libido and constipation, not to mention many other problems related to the mind. Spirituality will simply tell us to watch everything with alertness and accept all anxiety and suffering with grace. This is required more to become deeply aware of any unfortunate situation and instead of going into depression, take remedial measures with awareness, so that we can make quiet our disturbed mind with meditation. Through spirituality, we will be able to handle any unfavourable situation in a better and more serene manner rather than brooding over it or worrying unnecessarily. Isn't that simply amazing?

***

We exist in a world where science, technology, logic and reasoning play primary roles. That is why there has been so much progress in these fields. Therefore, we should also study, understand and experience spirituality too with a logical and rational mind rather than on the basis of blind beliefs in rituals and dogmas. I agree that the ancient scriptures form the foundation of our meaning and purpose in life. However, we should not blindly follow historical and time-worn traditions, which were laid down for people living during those ancient periods.

The ancient texts do provide the fundamentals of spirituality, but its comprehension, as time goes by, and the follow-up require regular upgradation. We should stop living in the past and desist from worrying about the future and live in the present. Apart from spirituality, what more is required is the association and participation with yoga, which has no connection to any personal God, religion or blind beliefs. Yoga believes purely in the practice of uniting the body, the mind and the spirit as one. Of late, yoga has made its mark almost all over the globe.

We should also perform meditation with awareness in the present moment; the essence behind this spiritual method is fully accepted by science today.

We should be religious in our acts but not rigid in following the tenets of religion blindly. We should relate to God not as a noun but as a verb; i.e., not as a person but as an experience in our acts of godliness.

A spiritual person is basically an atheist; he believes in the oneness of all, based upon the absolute, impersonal and supreme reality: the Para-Brahman. God is purely an inward experience, revealed in our acts of selflessness, compassion and oneness. We should first awaken to such an experience and realize that more than body and mind, we are the presence of that aware energy. Secondly, we should comprehend that our purpose is to experience dualities with a higher level of consciousness. Thirdly, we should accept that God, guru and the self are all one and not separate.

Chapter 30

THE IMPORTANCE OF SELF-REALIZATION

Our own self-realization is the greatest service we can render the world.
— Ramana Maharishi

Science and spirituality both claim that we are *not* body and mind; the former points to energy and the latter to the spirit. Both, in fact, mean the same; they only differ in their names. If we consider our thoughts, emotions and beliefs, besides our ego, desires and aspirations, we figure out that they do not fully represent who we are because these are transitory, short-lived and temporary; they come and go. What is long-lasting is the 'self', which refers to the subject of who we are. The self indicates we are not merely an object comprising body and mind but refers also to that subject, the eternal presence of our true identity.

***

In this journey of life, as the self expands, it evolves and seeks higher levels of knowledge in the subject of its unique individuality. The actual self is that spiritual path that we tread as we move from the material towards the spiritual; i.e., from the lower consciousness towards the higher consciousness. We gain a deeper insight into the core dimensions of what we aspire to realize. In simple terms, the self is the merging of body, mind and soul, representing its wholeness in totality as one.

There are three stages in the entire process of self-realization.

In the first stage, we need to comprehend the inner truth that we are more than our body and mind. Besides the thinking mind, there is also the presence of this unique spirit, which is aware and conscious of its own mind. Even though the mind mostly functions on its own unconsciously, individual awareness or the spirit characterizes us and sets us apart in determining, regulating and mastering what the mind does.

Only a human mind is conscious of its own motion, whereas other minds (of, say, animals) are not. Meaning, we are also aware of our own awareness: our mind has this ability to awaken that spirit embodied within in order to upgrade its own consciousness. This is what makes us different from all others as we grow, evolve and transform. We need to awaken and realize this personal inner truth of our individuality and also realize the real self, which indicates that we are, in reality, spiritual beings going through human experiences (as mentioned earlier).

***

The second stage begins after we awaken to the fact that, besides the cognitive mind, we also have the presence of another self: the spirit representing itself as that witnessing self. It guides our thoughts, words and actions and corrects them as and when they go astray. It is that soul residing within us, which is fully aware of the need to transform our consciousness in purity and take it in the right direction. It makes us aware of our own inner level of past awareness, through sheer watching and observing. This element of observation is what makes us human, elevating us above all other creatures. This soul has God within and has no connect with the duality separated by physical existence in the relativity-related aspects of our life.

***

The third stage comes when we comprehend that connect with the universal presence in our body, mind and soul as one. It is the process of uniting with the beyond, the transcendence of merging with the cosmic source of oneness in the absolute. It is that last stage where physical existence has no meaning and we are united as one with the wholeness of the universe. It is a journey of uniting the personal to the impersonal in pure subjectivity.

Thus, it is clear that, in life, we traverse from the first stage onwards; discovering the inner truth and being introduced to our unique self or the spirit.

***

In the second stage, we experience the power of the conscious witnessing self as the real 'we' in order to watch and witness our own level of awareness.

In the third stage, we connect the inner with the outer, the self with the universe as one in self-realization that both are the same as one absolute unit.

***

From the foregoing discussion, we come to know, experience and realize that we are not only body and mind but also the presence of a moving spirit of aware energy passing through various stages, which we refer to as life. This unchangeable, permanent ingredient is the core energy, which represents the force of our physical existence as the presence of our being in awareness.

Every force of energy requires a field to operate in and exhibit to realize its effect. In the case of humans, it is that field of consciousness, which we gradually build up through our experiential living during the course of our physical existence. The centre of our real Self comprises this emanating force of the spirit called awareness and its ambit is up to a particular boundary, within which it expands and evolves into its respective field and is called consciousness. This circle of life in totality forms our individuality as the self. As mentioned earlier, the state of its being is awareness and the state of its becoming is consciousness.

Accordingly, the self interacts through its power of awareness and experiences by means of its primordial consciousness journeying through life in the forms of child to ego to divine consciousness. It perceives and experiences everything using the body and the mind, existing in duality and transmitting neural activity through sense organs. In this manner, the unconscious body and the mind contain the personal aspects, whereas the conscious spirit becomes the impersonal or the transpersonal feature. All three unite and form in totality the outer and inner presence to experience and realize our actual self.

***

Spiritualism states that the passage of life needs to go through various phases embracing a series of experiences, as well as expanding and evolving from child to ego consciousness to divine consciousness in order to realize the true identity of the self. This journey begins from the permanent state of absolute energy in the form of the spirit taking on an impermanent form of dual energy comprising a gender within a body and a mind as matter and returning to recycle this pattern, which is called life.

***

According to spiritualism, the separated conscious spirit continues its journey, going through successive cycles of birth and death, until it becomes pure to self-realize the absolute in total awareness as to who and what it really is. It finally enters the unified field of universal consciousness, realizing its destination in the oneness of its absolute nature. This process, in totality, is referred to as self-realization.

***

Let us now study the feasibility of realizing pure consciousness or self-realization as claimed by spiritualism and whether it is really feasible or not. First, let us see what actually self-realization entails. For that, we also need to be clear on its meaning, which may differ from one person to another. It can mean fulfilment by oneself after being liberated from all worldly attachments and identities. It can also mean the death of our illusions in not being ego or mind by realizing that Creator within us.

We may also refer that to the oneness in unison with the absolute or the cosmic self. Meaning, we have risen from that 'somethingness' in body and mind into that nothingness of the universe, which within itself contains the fullness of all that exists. It can also be experienced in every present moment, when the mind is silent and we are in the absoluteness in unison with the ultimate reality.

Therefore, all these connotations basically converge into the oneness of who and what we are.

Now, if we consider the 'self' in a composite of all the three – body, mind and spirit – as one, then such a realization becomes a little unclear. The soul or the spirit will have to become independent from the other two that is the body and the mind, in order to realize its true self. In my opinion, we can only be *awakened* towards this ultimate self and may not realize the same, while we are awake and alive. In order to realize the impersonal and eternal soul, we will need to discard our body and mind; otherwise it would not be possible. The whole process becomes inconsistent, since it requires these three to be totally united with each other in equilibrium as one, *while we are alive, which is simply not possible.*

There are two views on this subject. The first denies the exclusive immortality of the human consciousness separating from the body and the mind after its death and entering another. According to this theory, the consciousness along with the body and the mind, as one composite unit, disintegrates and returns to its absolute state of nothingness as dormant energy of the universe.

The second view proclaims that consciousness or the soul can exist independently from the human body and the mind in eternity, for the sake of realizing its purity in order to regain its true identity, referred to as self-realization. Even though there are a few near-death testimonies by persons claiming that they could witness their souls leaving their bodies, it becomes hard for a rational mind to fully assimilate the view that the soul keeps moving from one cycle of birth and death to another for the sake of its true realization.

Despite philosophical affirmations, one feels that this sort of a claim (about the soul leaving the body) further leads to disillusionment and dissatisfaction with life. It makes us depend on an external God, who is supposed to be fully realized, coolly forgetting that God, who is residing within. It also lessens the value of the inner God, apart from splitting our personality into two and instilling fear in us with regard to the future. Such a situation leads to a contradiction, which restricts the body, the mind and the soul from experiencing and realizing their true identities, in this very life itself, whether they do so in totality with purity or not.

***

According to spiritualism, as mentioned earlier, all three, the body, the mind and the soul, are a part of the same absolute in different aspects. As per the doctrine of the supreme reality, all are one and not separate. In the oneness of the absolute, none of them can be independent or exclusive of each other; the spirit is fully embodied in the body and the mind to express its presence. On its own it represents nothing; the word 'nothing', in this case, implies the dormant state of the absolute in its purest form. It is only when the field of energy expands due to motion and leaves its core that it becomes active and dynamic. In the absolute stage, it remains in equilibrium and displays changeless passivity.

It is only when the intelligence energy of life goes into motion through physical matter that it activates the mind, which moves into a state of dual living in order to experience what this world is all about. The external material world becomes the cause for transcendence to uplift the consciousness to realize the inherent absolute God residing internally. Both are equally essential; it is only after experiencing one that the other becomes active. This is more to experience and realize vis-à-vis the totality of our being in this very life and not give exclusive rights to any one out of the three. It does not make any sense to claim that the soul detaches itself from its own absoluteness in this existence and presumes to experience the same in another.

From this absolute existent, all forms arise; therefore, neither the forms of the body and the mind nor the self or the world are in any way unreal. They are all real and accordingly express different characterizations of the absolute. Illusion (maya) is simply a psychic experience played out within us and is created by the cognitive mind functioning in duality. The power of maya can lead one's consciousness either towards divinity at one end and, if not, into the paradoxes of dual existence at the other. This power of maya is integral only to the human mind.

***

The foregoing cognitive experiences can lead us towards an illusory cycle of pleasure and pain through the 'me and mine' mentality. The reason is that the human mind may have the choice to experience, evolve and expand from either the divine or the devil and realize life to its fullness. In this manner, the body eventually reflects the condition of our mind, which, in turn, reflects the purity of our consciousness, depending on the path we wish to take.

***

All three, the body, the mind and the spirit dance in the field of maya, orchestrated unconsciously by the mind, eventually to return to its permanent, passive state of absoluteness, thereby terminating the optical illusion of physical existence. Life actually is but a defined motion of the absolute energy, experiencing physicality through its power of maya.

The real absolute self, simultaneously, also remains aloof from the cognitive mind, fully aware of what the other self is doing, functioning as the witnessing self. The image created by maya is like a veil hiding the truth of the absolute self. Since it cannot exist independently of the mind, one can safely presume maya also to be a part of the same absolute.

Therefore, the absolute energy in a human being has three aspects: the first as the real spiritual witnessing self; the second as the dual personality, materially existing in opposites; and the third as the illusory self in a false ego existing only within the thoughts of the mind. All three aspects simultaneously exist within every individual mind to represent the absolute experiencing what life is all about.

***

The purity of the soul remains intact, as the witnessing self, throughout one's existence whispering silently: 'Do not try to seek me in your next life.' The seeker (soul), seeking (mind) and the sought (object) are all one and the same, existing in 'the now'.

Let us now imagine the absolute speaking:

> I as the absolute have this privilege to experience life, exist with different aspects in the manner I deem fit. I am right here within your mind, experience and realize, if you can.
>
> Shake off the underlying impurities, embedded in the illusory aspect of dual existence, created by the mind. Do not devalue me by separating the soul from the body and the mind. I am that divine

within as much a part of your existence as the other two; realizing me is your objective. We are all one, exist as one and will rejoin as one, representing a single independent unit of the absolute.

I have liberally used the word absolute to elaborate on various spiritual connotations. In my view, the absolute is that principle of purity underlying the oneness of energy in totality and in addition to its existence as the one and only essential ultimate reality. It has been well defined by two principles: the ancient scriptures use the term 'Para-Brahman' and science as energy in its theories of quantum mechanics, both relating and referring to the same concept.

Para-Brahman happens to be the core belief in Hinduism. The Rig Veda (around 3500 years old) proclaims: *'The truth is one, but the wise describe it in many ways.'* It is that highest form, which is beyond all descriptions and conceptualization. It refers to that ultimate reality as the absolute aware energy, in which all other realities are an extension of this principle. By itself, it is changeless, but expresses itself in many changeable forms. It has many manifestations and the clearest is in the case of humanity: men and women. For this reason, we are a part of that divine absolute, and in order to relate with that principle, we (those who follow polytheism) do so by symbolizing it with a personal God.

***

It is for this reason that Hindus are permitted to pray to any manifestation of this absolute, whether it be a river, mountain, tree or any person with a higher consciousness. All this imagery of different Gods is but an expression of the same abstract principle in the form of the absolute. The principle and personality are restored to their oneness, reconciled in a human manner. The whole expression is frozen when one realizes and expresses the same as one and the only absolute and ultimate reality.

***

The ancient saints clearly explained the concept of reality in the form of Brahman, as the absolute supreme reality. It is the one and only existent, which penetrates and prevails in all that exists. However, due to multiple minds interpreting the same from complex ancient Sanskrit scriptures, the concept of spiritualism differs today from that of the olden times, with different views leaving the seeker to determine his own path in this journey of life.

***

With the passage of time, the supreme message of the Para-Brahman has been diluted; personal Gods have become more prominent in our lives, conveniently forgetting the impersonal God residing within us. It is to the personal Gods that we pray out of fear and convenience since they do not ask for anything in return. However, the inner impersonal One has a whole lot of demands, asking us to be selfless, fearless and compassionate, which we deftly avoid since these are hard to fulfil.

The ancient Sanskrit gems such as 'tat tvam asi' (thou art that) and 'Aham Brahmasmi' (I am the infinite reality) clearly indicate that the God and the self are within for us to experience and realize. We cannot escape from reality or awaken the soul by praying in religious places, thus isolating it from its other two parts (the body and the mind), and conveniently leave that for future births to experience on their own. In the journey of life, the soul demands to live in existentiality, meaning from one moment to the next, and the mind the other way round; from the past into the future. In the midst of this paradox, we exist to create our unique individuality, which, of course, may remain till eternity.

***

The ones with higher consciousness are actually those with strong individualities like Lord Rama, Lord Krishna, the Buddha and Jesus Christ, who left their legacies behind for all time to come. Their consciousness rose to such high intensities from their own personal awareness, not for seeking self-realization but to compassionately remain with us forever. Therefore, outside this very existence there exists only empty space in the form of dark energy comprising nothing, which is considered to be the infinite domain of the absolute self.

In that empty space made up of nothing, comprising 99.99 per cent space, we have some 5 per cent comprising the planets, consisting of living and non-living matter. Today, both science and spirituality have an identical view: all that exists in this universe is basically nothing. However, they also agree that we have something called energy, exhibiting its aliveness in different forms and fields from which the spirit/aware energy has been designated as the supreme form of human energy.

***

Every force and its respective field of energy keep on expanding and evolving, having no beginning or end. What we need to know in our study is what exists outside in the universe is exactly the same that exists inside our body, mind and soul. They are not separate; since there is only a single fundamental absolute energy expressing different features, which are in continuum with this infinite space referred to as the cosmos.

Author's Note

I have come far on my spiritual journey; yet there is so much more to learn. I hope you, my dear reader, will appreciate my viewpoints and ideas so you may understand how life and satisfied living take on a whole new meaning once you have embarked on this search for the truth.

This is only the beginning …

Acknowledgements

I wish to express my gratitude to all

- my friends who helped, with their critical analyses during the gradual progress of this book and
- my editors who went through the manuscript time and again, adding their inputs and substantially enriching the final result.

A deep and heartfelt appreciation to my family: my wife Komilla, who patiently overlooks my distracted nature while I am busy penning my thoughts, and to my daughters, Nadisha and Shreeya, who are my greatest critics.

I am forever grateful to my late parents, who laid the foundation of my scientific and analytical nature.

HAY HOUSE INDIA

Look within

Join the conversation about latest products, events, exclusive offers, contests, giveaways and more.

 Hay House India

 @HayHouseIndia

 @HayHouseIndia

 HayHouse.co.in

We'd love to hear from you!

www.ingramcontent.com/pod-product-compliance
Lightning Source LLC
LaVergne TN
LVHW091629070526
838199LV00044B/996